On the Edge of a Miracle

Be Blessed!
Hugh B. Shelton
My love to all.

Copyright 2017 – E. Amelia Billingsley
1st Edition
Published: Missions Support Services
Chestnut Mountain, Georgia 30502
All Rights Reserved
Printed in the United States of America

Rev. Hugh B. Skelton and Louise Skelton

Ministering in the Lord's service for over 60 years

A Note from the Author
E. Amelia Billingsley

I chose to tell this biographical view of the travels and ministry of the Rev. Hugh Skelton as though he were telling the story. It seems the better way to engage the reader in the activities and situations of the various countries. The information of the book was obtained through a multitude of documents, newsletters, and personal interviews. Rev. Skelton was totally involved in all aspects of the book, its content, and its publication.

It is not a light thing to travel the world in one's 80th decade of life. Preaching, teaching, and facing the difficulties of travel and foreign custom make the way even more difficult. Or, perhaps the better term is more "interesting". Rev. Skelton has enjoyed his journeys though some have been with trepidation and great effort. In following his call to "go into all the world and preach the Gospel..." (Mark 16:15), he provides us with fascinating stories and memories. It has been a delight for me to follow his path for the past few decades and to participate in many of his projects.

With the Rev. Skelton, we will walk "On the Edge of a Miracle," traveling to 5 continents and 30 countries from A to Z. Come and join us on the journey.

Special thanks to Jeanie Cassity, Martin Longstaff, Priscilla Sullins, and Weyland Billingsley

CONTENTS

Argentina	1
Aruba	5
Brazil	9
Chile	17
Costa Rica	21
Cuba	29
Dominican Republic	37
El Salvador	41
England and Wales	47
Guatemala	57
Guyana	69
Haiti	73
Honduras	77
India	87
Kenya	93
Medical Clinic	99
Mexico	105
Nicaragua	115
Nigeria	121
Panama	125
Peru	129
Romania	135
Russia and Ukraine	139
South Africa	147
St. Vincent	151
Thailand and Myanmar	155
Uganda	159
Zambia	163
Epilogue	167
Appendix	169

Argentina

"Where two or three are gathered together…"
(Mat. 18:20)

Argentina became familiar territory to me during the 1980's when I spent summers teaching in the churches there. With three other ministers, I taught the curriculum from our London school, the Center for International Christian Ministry (CICM), in a Spanish version. I was Director of the London school in the winter and helped teach the Spanish curriculum during the summer. Our "tour route" included Costa Rica, Venezuela, Paraguay, and Argentina. It was not until 2003 that I returned to Argentina with my son Allen and another pastor on a different mission.

In 2003, we were conducting evangelistic meetings and leadership workshops in the cities of Cipolleti and Neuquen in the southwest of the country and in Rosario in the northeast. It was a grueling schedule … three services daily and always local ministers and people wanting to talk, to share their victories and their challenges, seeking advice. They were hungry for spiritual communication. Congregations ranged in size from 60 to 500. It seems easier to speak to all the people possible in one service rather than have several repeated smaller ones. But, large crowds are more demanding on a speaker. Remember that ministry is not just "making a speech"

One service was rather unusual to me as I was asked to ordain the Superintendent of Churches as an "Apostle". It is the highest honor given to a leader in Argentina churches, and our host had met all of the 21 Biblical qualifications, including such things as spiritual leadership, planting new churches, uniting people in the faith, serving with humility yet defending the faith, etc. I was asked to be in charge of the ordination due to my senior status and my experience in worldwide ministry. I began by reading the requirements for apostleship. I then spoke to the audience about the credentials of this man. I reminded them that they knew him better than I did. He lived among them daily. They were well aware of his life and his ministry. It would be their duty to certify his status. "Is he qualified to be placed in this position and carry the title of Apostle?" Every person in the building stood signifying "yes". The new apostle received the honor humbly, and we rejoiced at the respect being shown to such a worthy servant of the Lord. True ministers of the Gospel do not serve for the accolades of the congregation. But it is uplifting to see people recognize excellence in their leader. It was a night of rejoicing and praise.

One evening, we attended an evangelistic service in the center of the city. It would be a revelation to me concerning prayer. The evening was terribly cold ... as in COLD!!! The services were being held in an open field, a sports field with bleacher seats. Masses of people sat in the open cold awaiting the service. I noticed two tents in the middle of the field. At first, I did not understand their use since they were not for attendees at the meeting. I later learned they were reserved for prayer after preaching.

The evangelist emerged from the small tent with a group of 150 followers and began the service. Speaking for only 20 minutes or so was all that was possible because it was just too cold to expect the audience to endure a longer sermon. It was in that short service that I learned the power of "the prayer of agreement". The 150 followers were prayer warriors. They took their places before the sermon began ... 50 women made a wall to the right of the minister, the other 50 women formed a line facing them. Behind the minister, 50 men made a semi-circle. These prayer warriors joined hands and quietly prayed throughout the sermon. They made no distracting movements nor any noise. They simply agreed in quiet prayer for the minister, the message, and the recipients.

The average number of conversions per service was 2000. When the call to prayer for salvation, for healing, and/or for deliverance was given, people seemed to pour toward the prayer tent. Inside that tent was a large circle of chairs, one for each person seeking prayer. As each person was seated, a counselor/prayer warrior stood before them and began to ask their need and lead them into a prayer to meet that need. Two prayer warriors stood behind the chair praying "We are in agreement with this prayer." Just praying in agreement for the presented need. It amazed me ... the power of the Prayer of Agreement. Hundreds claimed victory and gave praise to God for deliverance. And, I learned the lesson that "agreement of believers" is powerful beyond our imagination. It is not great words, celebrity speakers, or well-planned programming that brings people to Christ. It is the power of prayer. "For where two or three are gathered in my name, there am I among them."(Mat. 18:20)   The vision for the work in Argentina has grown over the years until today there is truly a positive outlook for their future

Aruba

"In the shade of the Divi Divi tree…"

After a pleasant flight, Louise and I stepped off the plane in Aruba and were stunned. I almost stumbled as I walked across the airport tarp and looked closely at the sign over the terminal door. Yes, it said "Aruba". But where were the palm trees, the beautiful flowers, the tropical views? Louise and I had expected the typical Caribbean island with visions of our beloved Cuba tucked in our minds. Not so. The beauty of Aruba is impressive, but it is not to be confused with lush tropical rain forests.

Lying just 16 miles off the coast of Venezuela in the Caribbean, Aruba is located in such a spot that it has summer the year around with a mild dry climate. The Trade Winds of the Caribbean keep it pleasantly warm but brush away harsh heat. It is a tourist paradise and the people of Aruba prosper as a result. No shanty towns or shabby houses spoil the landscape. THE industry of Aruba is tourism. Once known for gold deposits and oil production, the island now finds its major economic growth in tourists seeking the friendliness of the people and the white sandy beaches. People fly or boat in for the beautiful beaches and look for a place of shade under the Divi Divi trees so peculiar to the island. The tree spreads its broad canopy forming welcome shade on the southwestern side of the tree … always to the southwest where the winds have blown it since it was a sprout. The tree would be tall but again the wind has twisted its trunk and shortened it to form its spot of shade just over head high. The palm trees we had expected exist only in designed, planned spots ... all imported. So, life on Aruba was not what I had anticipated, but the surprises one encounters often surpass one's expectation of beauty. So it is with Aruba.

We made our first trip to the island in October of 2013 at the invitation of a local pastor whom we had met in Georgia at the General Conference of the Congregational Holiness Church. He invited us to come and teach leadership and preach in the local churches. It was a trip we would love to repeat. There were interesting services, beautiful scenery, and the kindest of people.

The history of the island has given it a unique language and cultural identity. The mixture of blacks, Caucasians and Asians has merged into a group of people who are now simply Arubans. Most of the people grew up with differing home backgrounds but merged into a single multi-cultural society where language variety is the norm. Historically, Aruba was ruled by English and then Dutch governments before its independence in 1986. Thus, the laws, languages, foods, and architecture of those countries are common elements of the nation. The legal system is entirely Dutch, and the European influence is much more evident than in other Caribbean areas. Spanish influences crossed the narrow water passage to the edge of South America years ago, leaving a large Latin culture. Philippine speech and culture was brought to Aruba by the many immigrants who come to work in the tourist industry. The result was church services in Spanish, English, Dutch, Filipino and the local dialect, Papiamento. In a single service, a song was sung in English, then again in Spanish, and perhaps again in another few languages. The sermon was translated into Papiamento or another common language. The Philippine service was usually held separately but with plenty of translations there also. In reality, most people have some fluency in five languages. The cultures as well as the languages mix constantly. There was always someone around who could translate for you whatever the conversation.

Our first service was in an exceptionally nice modern church named "Jesus Your New Hope Church". Average attendance was about 100-200. Services were very similar to those of the southern U.S. with lively keyboard and guitars leading the worship. Choruses were the favored music, using an overhead projector to keep the congregation involved. In the evening, we spoke in a Philippine church which we organized into a conference church later in our stay. In the same building, we taught a diverse group which included English/Spanish/Papiamento in the morning and Filipino/Papiamento in the evening.

For three days, I conducted leadership training classes which were well seasoned with questions, comments and conversations concerning just how to properly handle church problems, increase church growth, and involve the membership in the church. It was a delight to share my experiences and to learn of their faith. Hopefully, it was not my last trip to Aruba. The people are dedicated and energetic. And, the ocean beaches are not bad at all.

BRAZIL

"Two fried eggs for me, please." -- Hugh Skelton

Every year, December takes me to Brazil. My son, Allen, and I travel together ... wading not through jungles but through airports. Usually our destination is Fortaleza on the farthest eastern edge of South America. From Fortaleza, the west coast of Africa is closer than the U.S. Flights always require changes in Miami ... on to Manaus ...then to another airline taking us to the city of Belen... and finally into Fortaleza. And, of course, the planes get smaller and smaller at every change. Still, it is one of our favorite trips. The city of Fortaleza, sits on the ocean with beautiful beaches and scenic cliffs. Several million people are permanent residents of the city but the tourist population runs that number up to over a million each year. This is not the Amazon jungle or local communities scattered in the rain forest. Fortaleza is a city of high rise buildings and first class hotels ... a valued destination for European vacationers. The beach shopping mall has over 2000 shops ... a great place to buy cashew nuts and souvenirs to take home.

Although I first visited Brazil in 1972 in the area of Manaus, Allen first visited the Fortaleza area in 1996 and invited me along in 1998. We have gone together every year since then. However, I have to remember my place here. The people seem to have made a special place in their hearts for Allen, and he can do no wrong in their eyes. I'm the old man to be respected, but Allen is the young gun who makes them laugh and enjoy every session. He is the star of the show in Brazil. And, I don't mind at all. I just remind him on occasion that the Bible School in Fortaleza was named the Hugh Skelton Institute. (It is then he reminds me that his first name is actually Hugh.)

In 2013, the Assembly of God Church held its 50th Anniversary of the work in Fortaleza with a service beyond description. Over 15000 people were present with flags decorating the auditorium. Several choirs of over 100 persons sang songs of praise and worship. I was overwhelmed as I slid into my seat on the back of the platform filled with dignitaries and guests. Then, I was taken by the arm to the front of the group and was speechless as the group honored Allen and me for our work with them in Brazil. Plaques and a Bible were presented to each of us. I was overcome by the love and friendship of the Brazilian church. Even so, the treasures on this earth and the delight of sharing in the growth of Gospel churches does not compare to the joy we will share with our Brazilian family in the hereafter.

Few realize that Brazil is larger than the continental United States in size. In fact, it is the 5th largest country in the world. However, its culture and geography are far different from ours. The people seem to be either gathered in large metropolitan areas or spread in small jungle villages. Numbers of Brazilians live beyond roads, electricity, or television. On the other hand, millions live in large cities, near beautiful beaches, and have all the conveniences that we enjoy. But, I have always found individuals there to be kind and considerate … a giving people … people who love to laugh and sing and have fun.

One thing I don't enjoy in Brazil is casseroles. Yes! That's it. Their cuisine includes a lot of casseroles of fish and varied meats. They are well prepared and most find them delicious. My problem (which is a well-kept secret) is that I just do not care for casseroles anywhere ... even those Louise cooks. I eat casseroles to be polite, but I do not enjoy them. The kind people of Brazil often prepared meals for us or invited us into their homes. My oft made request was, "Two fried eggs for me, please." I eat a lot of eggs on mission trips, but I'm happy with that.

We usually arrive in Brazil on a Tuesday, take Wednesday to get settled and rest, and then spend four days with barely time to breathe. We are met at the airport by the general superintendent of churches and treated like royal visitors among lifelong friends. Allen and I are the "Fortaleza Tag Team" with two conferences running simultaneously. Allen speaks at the annual Assembly of God Conference while I teach at the Congregational Holiness Training Conference. The next night, we switch places, and I get his congregation of the night before and he gets mine. One group usually runs 350 plus pastors while the other is never under 600. In 2015, over 1000 were registered for the conference. It is exhausting. It is challenging. It is wonderful.

The conferences focus on pastoral training, church growth, and methods for motivating and teaching church members. We also take audience suggestions after each session and try to include them in the next session. Pastors want to know how to properly handle baptisms and tithing and especially how to pioneer new churches. Procedures for handling Eucharist (Communion) as well as integrity both in the pulpit and among the congregation are major concerns. My favorite question always seems to come up somewhere .... "Rev. Skelton, can you tell us some stories of what you have learned in your 68+ years of ministry?" I just take a deep breath and depend on something useful to come to mind. It is good to learn from those who have gone before us and who have more experience than we do, but it also a fact that every person ministers as their gift and their circumstances permit. We can learn from others and prepare ourselves, but we also have to just jump in and "swim" sometimes.

In addition to the evening services and some day sessions as well, we visit churches spread throughout the vast city. With some 30 churches, we usually try to visit two each day. There is no time for rest because another visit or another service is never more than an hour away. For the country of Brazil, Fortaleza is an evangelical energy center of a Brazilian state that is almost as large as the state of Georgia. Cities and villages throughout the state of Ceara send representatives to the conference. They are back home repeating our teaching in their local churches almost by the time Allen and I fall asleep on the plane home.

Fortaleza, Brazil, has become our December trip. It is the one time of the year that I get to spend time and work closely with my son. But, it was not here that I got my first introduction to Brazil. Allen was less than a teenager when I first visited the jungle area of Manaus, Brazil. In 1972, I traveled to one of Brazil's most interesting cities with new missionaries, Rev. L. M. Reese and his wife, to begin their missionary effort along the Amazon and tributary rivers. Manaus is centered in the middle of the Amazon rainforest and is accessible only by airplane or boat. But our churches in the area now stretch for 1600 miles up and down the Amazon River and into its tributaries. Travel to visit the churches is irregular because of frequent flooding, but each church has a local pastor and is well attended. As the center of many Amazon tribes, Manaus sends boats of all sizes into the jungle area on a daily basis. Just catch a boat, hang your hammock on deck and stow your bag underneath it. Be sure to take plenty of water and food ... either that or a fishing pole.

Rats, mosquitoes and boat trips...they always remind me of the Amazon area. We literally had to scrape the layers of mosquitoes from our arms traveling up the Amazon. And, despite every effort to eliminate them, rat infestations are frequent. I well remember a night long past when I awoke to find I had slept with two rats in bed with me. Our trip to Manaus and up the Amazon in the 1970's brought fewer rats, but more mosquitoes. It was one of our first trips upriver for Louise and me with 12 others traveling inland to dedicate a church.

We rented a boat for the trip from Manaus from a local boat rental. It arrived about 1 o'clock in the morning and unloaded its cargo. We then took our small bags of personal items and climbed to the top deck. The boat started upriver with a lot of noise, strong exhaust fumes and a crew member at the front, constantly shining a spotlight to look for floating logs that would wreck us. As we strung our hammocks on the top deck, we took care to make sure there was room for all and to find a way to remember which was ours. We had one cot, but everyone else slept in individual hammocks. The trick was to get them all to swing the right direction so we would not bump into one another. Thus, we all crawled in at sleep time and counted "1-2-3 swing right". Once we all got to going in the same direction, the boat motion kept us on track.

The boat trip had taken 20+ hours to reach the jungle village. The return would be only a little shorter. After the brief visit and church dedication, we boarded a boat to get back to Manaus. Things did not go well on that voyage. When we unpacked, we discovered that some of the crew had stolen several items from our bags during the night. As we unloaded in Manaus, one of our group members lowered our one cot over the side of the boat. A man passing by ran over and grabbed the cot and ran. Not to be outdone, our man jumped off the boat and chased the thief down the street and forcefully took our cot back. The experiences of mission travel are seldom common "tourist trips", and I for one am thankful for resourceful people to travel with me.

On another trip, our boat decided to do whirls in the water. A storm, not unusual for the Amazon, broke the chain on the motor driving us and providing steering. We began to spin in the turbulent waters and finally stopped at a dead tree stump to which we quickly tied the boat. Whew, finally sitting still. NO ... the storm was violent enough to tear the tree stump from the river bank. Again, we began to spin. Thankfully, our missionary finally got the chain reattached so we could continue. Some missionaries have to be mechanics and others, like me, have to pray in time of trouble. It was an unforgettable experience, but one that reminds me of the goodness of the Lord, even in the midst of a storm.

The churches in Brazil now number over 200 with more than 10,000 members. In February 2015, we made a joyful return to Manaus. The general superintendent of the Congregational Holiness Church in Brazil had called a conference for all fellow pastors and workers in South America. It was the first such meeting of the leadership from all our church conferences in South America. Representatives came from almost every nation in the church family, even from Aruba in the Caribbean. The city of Manaus became the scene of a really big family reunion...family that had just met in the natural but were instantly related spiritually. Over 300 representatives from 10 different nations sang together in unison, choosing their own personal language of Spanish or Portuguese or English. Customs differed from country to country but no one really noticed. Services were done in both Spanish and Portuguese for day and night sessions. Six from the U.S. attended and I was quite busy interpreting as I and a church brother from Aruba were the only ones able to speak all three needed languages. We were kept busy between services, translating for shopping and general conversations. It was my honor to be speaker for the Sunday morning service.

And, we even did a little sight-seeing together. Boats can easily take a short ride down the Black River (Rio Negro) to join the Amazon and thus access the eastern seaports of Brazil and, indeed, the entire world of shipping. Manaus was a city of wealth when the rubber from the forest trees was valued throughout the world.

But, synthetic rubber slowly robbed the great city of its major business. Today, it is a waning city of two million showing its historic side to tourists and lazily remembering its better days of success. Still, the grand opera house of Manaus calls back to those days of glory. But our outing for the day was on the river. We secured a rental boat to travel down the Rio Negro to where it met the mighty Amazon. It was a much better trip on the tourist boat than the one in my memory from my first visits to Manaus. Back in town, we walked as new found friends through the city, touring the famous opera house and helping each other bargain in the market for that perfect souvenir that shouted "Brazil" when hung on our wall at home.

As the men and women of the conference returned to their home countries, we could see clearly the progress of the ministry throughout Mexico, Central America, South America, and the Caribbean. My trips to Fortaleza each year will continue and perhaps we will visit Manaus again. Over the years, I have traveled thousands of miles throughout the country of Brazil, visiting and establishing churches. After 60 plus years of missions ministry, I now cherish every mile traveled.

Chile

But my God shall supply all your need according to his riches in glory by Christ Jesus." (Philippians 4:19)

I've never been disappointed with the beauty of the country or the zeal of the people of Chile The narrow country that runs for more than 2500 miles down the west side of South America has a long coast line and a backbone of Andes mountains. With sandy beaches and access to ski resorts only miles apart, Chile is an ideal place for adventurers and nature lovers. Industries flourish, especially the grape industry making Chile world famous for its wine. Job opportunities are plentiful and the people prosper more than many South American countries.

In the 1980's, I visited Chile on an annual basis, traveling to Chile to teach our CURSOM classes on leadership and church growth. In those days, I traveled with two missionary friends, and we taught what had been our London curriculum in Spanish. One person we met during those times was a Methodist pastor with the most incredible church building I have ever seen. The church housed some 17,000 people at times and took one whole year of around the clock construction to complete. The most amazing thing was the roof. The metallic dome spread over the entire church with only its edges touching the outside walls. How could they keep it suspended like that? The pastor explained that Chile is known for more than its share of earthquakes. To guard against a destructive quake, engineers designed an "airplane like" roof. It was made from the metal of airplanes and somehow "floated". This meant that when the walls shook from a quake, the roof would not fall. Amazing! It was beauty and security all in one.

During my days as Superintendent of Missions for the Congregational Holiness Church, our work in Chile began. Allen, Jose Rubio, and I went down to meet with a local church that had no denominational connection. That small Santiago beginning has now grown to encompass twelve established churches and several missions' stations in the countryside. However, we were not prepared to be cold. Somehow, we failed to remember that seasons are opposite in the Southern Hemisphere, but we remembered it immediately when we stepped off the plane. First stop ... coat shop for warm jackets, gloves and head covering.

Services in Santiago were always exciting. They were warm in spiritual content and fellowship, but not in temperature. I'm not sure if the 25 people who came in were there to hear the Gospel or to get warm. Services were similar to ours in the states with a few additions. When it was time for service, those present went out into the street in groups, inviting people in. When all had gathered back, the service started. Services were lively with plenty of music and an occasional cry of "Will you be kind enough to close that door?" after someone entered and left the door ajar.

In 2006, we took a group to Chile to dedicate a church in the mountains built in the name of our longtime friend, Garvis Elliott. His wife and daughter joined us with several other ministerial friends. Though we visited several churches along the way, our goal was a mountain village. The plane trip from Atlanta can be an eight hour direct flight with no flight delays or changes. Upon arrival, our agenda was nap first and then a visit to our first church in the city for service. We were greeted at the service with delight and a delicious meal. We were a happy group ... until we saw the bus we were to ride for the next 10 hours. The trip south of Santiago was extremely beautiful, and the roads were so windy that we saw most things twice. The mountain roads, cool damp breezes, and hard seats made us aware that this was the mission field, not a vacation tour.

Of course, it is always important to take care in any country with large cities. One of our brethren learned that the hard way. One evening he returned to the hotel very excited and telling of the new camera he had bought. He had been offered what he knew to be an expensive camera by a street vendor. At first, he passed it by but then realized that for $60 or so, he could have a $500-$600 camera. He returned and examined the camera closely. It was what he thought it was and seemed in perfect working order. He made the deal and the seller offered to put it in a sturdy bag for him. He waved the bag before us and sat it down to show us his purchase ... a sack of dirt! The switch had been made when the seller bagged it for him. Of course, when he returned to the seller, there was no one at that spot. Fortunately, he could laugh about his error, but we all re-learned the lesson. Whether in New York City, Atlanta, or Santiago, Chile, deals that are "too good to be true" usually are just that.

Sermon: It was in Chile that the Lord gave me one of my greatest sermons. I was asked to speak at a major service at the main church in Santiago and to serve

Communion to the congregation. The Lord placed on my heart a sermon I shall never forget. On the way to church, I asked our driver to stop for me to buy two loaves of bread. One I sliced into twelve pieces and the other I left whole. After introductions and appropriate Scripture reading, I began to present the slices of bread with an attribute assigned to each of them. The bread of "grace", "love", and "mercy" were followed by "forgiveness", "peace", "joy", "power", "healing", "signs and wonders", "miracles", and "whatever your personal need may be".

I talked with them about how the Lord desired to meet all our needs and how the ceremony of Communion was one avenue for making our requests and needs known to the Lord. Every person could have what he or she needed. Just choose your slice and commit that need to the Lord.

It was a well-received message. But then I brought out the other loaf....the one I had left whole. "Or, you can have the entire loaf," I said. "Our God is not a small God. He can and will supply whatever you need without limit." It is a truth I never forget. God will supply our needs if we ask and obey Him. Never think you have to choose your blessing. You can have the whole loaf if that is what you need.

COSTA RICA

The solid rock of Central America

Land of beaches and volcanoes ... democracy and "red tape". It is also a land where I spent three days in a jungle without a change of clothes. The airlines lost our luggage so we wound up as a group of ministers in grey shirts that were once white. Another time, we found ourselves in Turrialba with no hotel options. The only thing available was a bar with rooms on the second floor. The result was a full night of mosquito fight to the sound of loud rock music. But, we had clean shirts.

Still, the graciousness of Costa Rica is without parallel, and its status as a world leader in democracy is well earned. The Caribbean Ocean on one side, the Pacific Ocean on the other, and beautiful rainforests climbing up to volcanic peaks that belch sulphur fumes quietly. Costa Rica is indeed a jewel in the Central American chain. Its leadership in the areas of democracy, economic growth, in plant and animal species, and in level of personal income is unmatched in the area. Costa Ricans (Ticos) speak with pride of their abolition of a military presence, their education system that has produced a 97% literacy rate, and their overall stability.

And, though it is a paradise to live in and to visit, for missionaries it is also a country leading the "red tape" parade. They are not anti-religion, but the government is very protective of its citizens and regulates outside interests. An historic past of banana barons taking advantage of the work force and the land has made them wary of any outside group that might misuse their privileges.

Our success in Costa Rica began in the '60's when I drove down from McAllen, Texas, with two young missionaries. They settled in the capital city of San Jose and enrolled in the Spanish language school which is respected world-wide. Since then, the church has gone through cycles of growth, contraction, and now stable growth. So, in 2003, I was back on the road...no, I was in the air, headed for the mountains of Costa Rica.

With only two disruptions, Costa Rica has maintained its sovereignty and democratic government since the late 1800's. After one of those disruptions in 1949, they completely demilitarized. Costa Rica has chosen democratic solidarity over the charismatic leadership style so common to Latin American countries. Their beautiful beaches on both coasts compare to any country in the world and have helped make it a tourist mecca. A few hours flight from the U.S. puts you on flawless beaches, forests of wild life and zip lines, tropical food and drink delights, sunshine, and as Louise says "Lots of coffee ... good coffee!"

Just check the travel section of your Sunday newspaper for plenty of "deals" to Guanacaste and San Jose. Drive the highways in your rental car and enjoy the cleanly kept, white washed houses surrounded by well-kept shrubbery reflecting the pride of the "Tico" population. It is indeed an ideal vacation spot. But my trips were not vacations designed to enjoy the all-inclusive beach resorts. They were trips to fellowship with the Christians of Turrialba and the highlands...prime examples of the considerate and kind Costa Rican people.

The church group had grown from its beginnings and eventually settled in the mountain areas around Turrialba about a 45 minute drive from San Jose. In 2003, several ministers accompanied me on a visit to the area. In the mountain towns of Siquirres and Cartago, we taught in several of the local churches Siquirres lies a bit past the Turrialba volcanic region and our second area of churches. Cartago is located back toward San Jose but through winding mountain gaps.

Topics for our seminars in those cities included Basic Leadership, Soul Winning, and Strategies for a 21st Century Church. The journey into the mountains was tiring but the reception was very satisfying. Each session drew from 50 to 300 participants. Again I was often asked just to share what I had personally learned in my many years of mission's work. They wanted practical information ... things they could put into use to be better pastors and leaders.

By 2011, the church population in Costa Rica had grown a great deal. Some difficult years of legal adjustments and even a split among members of the conference took a toll, but the overall work continues to prosper. Much of the difficulty in Costa Rica arises from government regulation, the regulation aimed at preserving the leadership of local person but actually creating difficulty in keeping all the paper work current to maintain building permits and legal documents. We do not conduct medical clinics in Costa Rica. Taking medications into the country is not permitted by the government. The country has its own medical program which far exceeds most Central American countries, and they feel that protection for their population is provided by regulating medication quality. This protection from external medicines has valid basis after several incidents of improper medications in some countries. It makes life both wonderful and difficult for the "Ticos". Despite these problems, it is good to see a government that takes the welfare of its citizens as a prime responsibility. The government is protective but still very open to advanced training and evangelism in the churches.

I made this trip to check the status and needs of the churches and to visit with old friends. Our local church leader showed up at the airport, and we began a pleasant drive up to the city of Turrialba. The week went like this:

Thursday: SEMINARS: We held seminars in one of our newer churches teaching on leadership as well as church development. Then the local pastors of the area gave their reports for about two hours. The reports were cause for rejoicing and made the whole day a pleasure. I noted that the church where we had service was using a rented building and prayed with the congregation for a building to purchase.

Friday: CHURCH VISITS: A major goal in this type of missions travel is to visit with as many local pastors and leaders as possible. I try to evaluate the work for growth potential, and to determine the needs of the churches, both physically and spiritually. Second only to preaching is my delight in discussing the work with these "front line" warriors. I am often called upon for advice but always learn from them. On this Friday, we rode through the mountains, into several smaller towns to meet and renew friendship with pastors and their families. The "Ticos' take good care of their properties with white washed houses and well-kept shrubbery. They do no less with their churches. In early U.S. years, circuit riding preachers often got saddle sores from their constant travel. I guess I can only claim a little car seat discomfort.

Saturday: FOOD DISTRIBUTION AND YOUTH RALLY: This was a day for the youth. In the morning, we spent two hours with the children's food ministry. Food was given to over 40 children. And, Louise did what has always been her special talent. Most of our pioneer church work began with the Louise establishing Sunday School classes among the children. It was those classes that provided our first inroads into new areas. . It seemed only natural for her to set up a Sunday School lesson for the 40 plus their mothers. The class had a good response as over 30 prayed with her at the end. It was a time of rejoicing before a quick stop to rest for the next service. Evening took us to a slightly older group ... the teens and young adults of the church. What a service! The young people took charge of a well-organized but lively service with special presentations of artistry and music. I almost wore my shoes out patting my foot to the music from their lively guitars, keyboards, drum and other musical instruments. These young people enjoy their church. I was privileged to speak to them for the evening sermon. I chose Matthew 13:38 as a basis for my comments on "The World is the Field". My challenge to them was that they should become leaders who influenced the world and brought the light of Christianity to all they met. The youth responded with enthusiasm. I realized that this group had a lot to give to a world in need, and I believe they will answer the challenge of their generation. A wonderful day ... but a tiring one. Bedtime was welcome that night.

Sunday: CHURCH SERVICE: We spent Sunday in the normal format. I spoke in local services and enjoyed meals with old friends. We combined personal social activity and spiritual conversations. It was a more restful day than the past few or the ones to come.

Monday: BANANA LAND: Our last day of ministry took us down from the volcanic mountains to the Caribbean coast area of Limon known as a center for the country's banana history. From 1871 into the 1930's, United Fruit Company ruled that coastal area of Costa Rica. It was a plantation system at best with the company giving work to people who were without income, providing schools and health facilities, but taking it all down when they had depleted an area and were moving on. United Fruit left the area under political pressure. Today, Limon offers beautiful beaches and tourist activities in addition to well-managed banana production. Just say, "Thank you, Costa Rica" the next time you bite into your Chiquita banana.

But our main task was visiting with churches and with the pastors in the area. It was a delightful day ... clouded only by an awareness that our evening and Tuesday were going to be difficult. We were at or farthest point from the capital, San Jose, and the ride back took quite a while.

Tuesday: HOME: Having arrived late at the hotel, we tried to catch some sleep but 3:20 am started our day. We took a Taca Airlines flight to San Salvador, then to Miami, and then a domestic flight to Atlanta. That's the way a week on a mission trip goes. A daily mixture of activity and a bundle of plane and vehicle rides. It does take a few days to recover.

Every field of labor has its difficulties and its advantages. The difficulties in Costa Rica come from a sincere governmental interest in the welfare and health of its citizens. The advantages are fantastic people with leadership skills, a zeal for the Gospel, and a willingness to work for a victorious future for the church. It is a place of beauty and opportunity.

CUBA

"First Love"

Yes, Cuba will always remain my first love in more ways than one. It is the land where I first committed to missions, but it is also where I first began to realize that Louise Skelton would become first in my heart. In 1951, I visited my sister, Dorothy, and her mission work in Santiago Cuba. Louise was there to help, having left her bed in a tubercular hospital. God's call to her was real and immediate. She had no doubts as to what was to be done. Though her family was not all pleased at her decision, Louise knew this was God's call.

I had known her most of my life but never thought of her as a future wife. During my one week visit to Cuba that changed dramatically. By the time I left, I was rather certain that a marriage proposal was in our future. I returned to the states to finish my education and to marry Louise. We would return in 1955 to work for six years in Cuba. During the early part of the revolution, one of Castro's leading generals told me, "We have your city surrounded. We know which house is yours. If we have to burn the city of Santiago for the sake of the revolution, we will burn it." They did not burn the city, but eventually did take control. I sent Louise and our son Allen back to the U. S. for safety, but stayed myself until a notice of criminal arrest was nailed to my front door. I had become a "wanted man" because of my religious work and my American citizenship. Without even a chance to return home and see the notice, I miraculously escaped the island

and headed to Florida. It is because of those legal issues that I have never been able to return to Cuba. Recent inquiries indicate that the warrant for my arrest is still on record. With the new moves to mend the relationship of Cuba and the United States, I hope for resolution to my problem. I want to return to my first love.

We left Cuba with 21 active churches, 44 Sunday Schools, and over 50 trained church workers. Having been a bit ahead of my time, our church work was well in the administrative hands of local pastors. For that reason, the organization outlasted Fidel Castro and still has over 47 active congregations today. Our efforts to support the work in those early days were like a spy novel. We deposited a set amount of money in the American bank account of a high ranking Cuban. He then released the amount in Cuban money to our local church superintendent. Every month, I awaited a telegram that would refer to some success, usually with an amount involved. Example: "We visited with a group of 100 young people in San Luis." That would mean they had successfully received the $100 for that month. In later years, a personal friend and minister from Mexico was able to travel to Cuba to encourage the work and help them financially. My son has also been able to go. And, even Louise made the trip.

So the Cuba story of today is Louise's story. She has been able to return to Cuba twice. Her first trip centered in a small town near Havana, the second took her to our old home area of Santiago. A church near Havana was sponsoring a Women's Aglow Conference, and Louise was invited to join seven other women on the trip. Having missed the plane in Miami, they arrived later than planned and were held up at the Havana airport. They had sent $50 per person in advance for "religious visas". Anyone expecting to speak at a church meeting is advised to have the "religious" permit. However, no one showed up at the Havana airport with the visas. After a long embarrassing wait, the officials offered them regular tourist visas at a cost of $15 each. No one objected to paying the fee immediately and getting out of the airport. A couple from the distant city of Santiago had come to Havana and provided transportation. Our local contact refunded the "religious visa" fees that she had been unable to obtain. Of course, the ladies managed to return the funds to the Cuban church in the form of offerings and gifts.

The American group divided up and went to stay with different local families for the days of the conference. Louise and her partner stayed in a small 5th floor apartment with a Cuban lady and her daughter. No elevator meant they got plenty of daily exercise. Though their host was attentive and kind, the situation in the home was troublesome. Opening the pantry showed three potatoes, one carrot, and an onion ... nothing more. The evening meal was a pasta with some sort of meat flavoring added. There was no complaint, but it was evident that there was no other food resource. The visiting ladies also noted quickly that there was no iron for their suit case wrinkled dresses. The process of laying clothes on the bed and smoothing them with one's hands just didn't really do the job. The Cuban people had only as much food as the government rationed for them each month. And, extras had to be bought with the small amount given each citizen every month. The ladies made a quick trip to the grocery store to buy food, an iron, and other things needed in the household. They searched the markets several days for some eggs but were unable to find such a prized item. That which is just basic necessity to people in our country is often luxury in Cuba.

At another time, Louise joined a group from north Georgia on a trip to Santiago, Cuba. This was "home" to her, the city where our ministry had centered, where we had lived and shared friendships with neighbors and church members. It was exciting to go back, but there were also thoughts of anxiety. Fear is not a problem when one rests in the assurance that the Lord is directing your path. But there was uncertainty about the problems of moving through customs and immigration. Would we have trouble entering the country with the medicines, clothes, cameras and a computer that we were carrying to our Cuban friends? How much will the country have changed in our many years of absence? The worries were in vain. A miraculous walk past custom officials was little more than a question or two and a nod. Outside the terminal, the sun shone brighter as the Superintendent of our church work on the island, Andres and his wife, Dorkas, greeted us. Indeed a number of old friends crowded around for hugs and laughter and "Gracias a Dios." It was good to be "home."

The following days in Santiago were filled with activity ... so many old friends to visit, so many new friends to get to know. Much had changed, yet much remained the same. Buildings were simply older. They had been well cared for but no major repair or new construction appeared. The collapsed economy of Cuba was evidenced by empty shops and a scarcity of merchandise. Food and clothing were rationed per household. A strict allowance of rice, beans, eggs and milk was enforced. The fresh fruit and vegetable vendors who crowded the streets in older times simply did not exist. Cuba was a country under Communist control with the average household struggling for food and clothing.

But, the average American tourist is mesmerized by the beautiful antique cars. The roads of Cuba are not crowded with cars even in the city. Horse drawn wagons, ox carts, large stake bed trucks serving as "stand up" taxis, and motorbike "coco taxis" provide the majority of transportation. But, the cars that do remain are vintage American from the '50's and '60's. Fresh paint, shiny wax and a good bit of "bondo" to fill cracks and dents provide a movie feel to a night out to dinner. The Cubans are genius at repairing and remaking parts for the old cars. Other than a small number of Russian Ladas, the auto supply for the island stopped when the Castro regime took control. Yet, just looking at an amazing '59 Chevy convertible, shiny and bright, speaks of the creativity of the Cuban people and their ability to adapt and improvise. Life has been difficult under Communism, but the people have survived. The smiles are still there. The music still fills the streets. Their kindness still spills from their hearts.

Two things in Cuba had improved in our absence. Education had become a priority with the Castro regime. Schools spread to the countryside and were open to all students. College study became free to all who could pass entry exams and every effort was made to provide training for those who did not. The Cuban people were well educated. The other segment of the Communist society to profit was the medical field. All people had access to doctors and medical care. Every block was assigned a doctor whose responsibility was to care for those within his or her territory. Medicine and medical care was being provided to all without cost. The one flaw was a major lack of medications and equipment, especially in small towns. Many areas had only minimal medications and depended on natural and herbal treatments. Hospitals were sparsely furnished and often crowded. But medical care and education were universally available.

The church in Cuba was neither discouraged nor saddened by the difficulties of daily life. The ladies attended services every evening ... services filled with music and dynamic preaching. And, they left with spirits uplifted knowing they had been in the presence of anointed worship and praise. The positive attitude of the people was amazing. The church that we had begun in Santiago was still open for service, but the roof was in disrepair. Louise was able to leave money to repair the roof. In San Luis, she found the church in excellent condition, having had excellent care over the years. The visiting group was also able to give the Superintendent of the Cuban Church a computer to open better communications with him. After almost 50 years, the seed sewn in Cuba still bore fruit. As one brother expressed the sentiment of the people, "They can take away our cars and 'stuff', but they can't take away our Jesus." The Cuban church has gone through fires of great persecution and suffering, but they have "come forth as PURE GOLD."

Leaving our Cuban friends was a time of sadness, but we rejoice in the hope that we will not wait so very long before we can visit. As political relations improve, we hope for free movement to visit our churches and to rejoice with them in their victories. "Viva la Cuba! Viva el Espiritu Santo que reina en la gente de Cuba."

> **Note from a Cuban friend**
> *"The Lord Jesus cover you with blessings. We always remember you with much love. We believe that God sent you to Cuba to save our large family. If you had not come to Cuba, we would be lost in darkness. Great are the mysteries of the Lord. We would not have known about Jesus if it had not been for you. Thanks be to the Lord for the time you spent in Cuba preaching the Gospel of love and salvation of the soul. I ask the question: What would have happened to me if I had not known the beautiful way of the Lord? We have difficulties, but the Lord is by our side. We have His promises and we hope in them. My family is all united in the church for which I give praise to my God. We appreciate you and we love you in Christ the Lord.*
> ~~ *Nenita*

Dominican Republic

"Come over...and help us." (Acts 16:9)

My arrival at the airport in Santo Domingo was quite normal. I took my time getting off the plane, stood in line to have my passport inspected, waited for luggage and headed out to meet the rest of our group. We were on one half of an island known for beaches and vacations, but we were not there for pleasure. It was a medical missions trip focused on delivering medical assistance to the poor. Our plane landed on the bright side of the island of Hispaniola, but there was a darker side. Life on the island is divided in every way. There are two countries, two cultures, two attitudes. And, ministry there has two sides ... a bright side of opportunity and a dark side of conflict and poverty.

The Dominican Republic has developed as a culturally friendly area with its economy fed by tourists coming down for short all-inclusive stays and beach holidays. Religious freedom is apparent with many evangelical churches, but there are also a large number of citizens who cling to their Creole roots and religion. The capital city is a mecca of English speaking tourists intent on relaxation. The diverse crowd includes many Germans and Europeans who enjoy their sun bathing with clothing and without. But beach time was not what we came for. Our focus would take us to the poorer parts of the island, to the border with Haiti.

Our pick-up truck headed inland toward the Haitian border, an area crowded with Haitian refugees seeking to survive the devastation that weather had done to their country. We all climbed onto the bed of our pick-up truck and sat on wooden benches. A tarp had been attached as cover to protect us from wind and possible rain. We huddled ... yes, huddled ... uncomfortably, unsure of what lay ahead. Our view out the back of the truck showed us only heavy traffic with numbers of farm trucks. We had left the comfort of taxis and enclosed vans behind us. We were now a quiet group on a mission trip. Road noise and constant dust discouraged any desire to carry on conversation.

While the Dominicans fight the crowds for sale items and beach space, the Haitians struggle to deal with food shortages, earthquakes, and political corruption. For that reason, large populations of Haitians settle themselves just over the border into the Dominican. They sit as refugees awaiting chances to return home or visit family. It was a desperate group of people trying to get what they could to survive. Among these "refugee" groups, we set up our first clinic.

I stood at the gate before the clinic began and said a brief prayer under my breath. "Lord, protect us. Let us help these people but keep us safe." The gate opened and the rush began. Pushing and shoving forward, each person wanted to be first to the medicines. Stopping for spiritual clinic or for medical evaluation was not on their minds. I quickly took a step back from what seemed like a shopping mall rush for a special sale. It took all our resources to establish a routine for spiritual clinic, conference with a medical professional, and medication distribution. The pushing and shoving of the crowd was almost frightening. Crowd control ... we needed it badly.

Our normal clinic set up was almost overrun by pressing Haitian refugees. My normal responsibility to provide a spiritual clinic aimed at presenting the Gospel and providing prayer for salvation, healing, or any specified needs was in jeopardy. These were people in need and "talk" was not their goal.

We were fortunate to have numerous local assistants who understood the best way to deal with things. They took over and restored some order to the clinic process. A blessing in the Dominican is that the evangelicals of the island are a group in unity. Denominational difference is set aside to meet the needs of the people. These local people saved our efforts and kept some appearance of order. Still, the entire day was a tiring struggle that would be repeated several times that week. The ministry was difficult, but the people were no less worthy than any other group. We minister to those most in need, not to the easiest.

I must admit I left the island basking in the delight of so many local Christians anxious to help where needed. I also left close to exhaustion. The clinics were as tiring and frustrating as they were fulfilling. After trips in 2007 and in 2009, I concluded that our overall success was limited. Our clinics were not effective as spiritual training or medical care. They were more like a "medicine hand out" booth.

The Dominican people are giving and helpful, but the government raises road blocks rather than smoothing pathways for the work. The civic leaders take little responsibility for the Haitian emigres huddled at their border, providing none of the government services supplied for the Dominican population. As a parting gift on our second clinic trip, the authorities at the airport confiscated four of our suitcases. Of course, they did not tell us this until we had checked the bags and were on the plane ... a bitter pill to swallow at the end of a hard week. I am sure the contents made it to the "black market" by the next day. Government interference makes the battle so difficult that a return to the area is not likely.

El Salvador

"Always expecting the unexpected."

"Danger" ... It's the first word one thinks of in connection with El Salvador. I can hardly forget the two times I got as far as the capital city of San Salvador and was refused entry because of the Civil War that raged. It was the year 2000 before we finally landed with a medical ministry team. The country has a history of social and psychological wounds due to centuries of oppression and over a decade of civil war struggles to find normalcy. The old web of violence, suspicion, and suffering is just beginning to heal. Where revolutionary militants were once were cause for concern, drug lords and gangs now present even worse danger.

Our first meeting with the church leadership in El Salvador was held in Guatemala at a service station. They wanted to work under our auspices though we could not personally enter their country. "El Salvador" literally means "the Savior" and through strong local leadership a renewed vision for increase and unity in the church was underway.

Our church group in El Salvador has deep roots. After their elder superintendent forged a strong church base, the Cantu family continued the ministry with strong effective leadership and a vibrant group of believers. They have an energetic congregation with an evangelical focus, striving to bring Christ to their neighbors. Still, the church needs more training to deal with the scars of past conflict. The lack of finance and insufficient staff present a constant hardship.

> **Lines from Louise...**
> On our first trip to El Salvador, I met my mother. Well, not really my mother but a lady who looked just like my mother. An elderly lady of 80 had helped establish the church in San Salvador, had dealt with sickness and conflict, but still stood beside her daughter as they focused on the church needs. Seeing her brings back memories of the woman who raised 12 of us children, always directing us toward the Lord.

After much prayer, the Lord opened the door/border for us to work with the Salvadoran church side by side. The first successful entry into the country was with a medical clinic. We took plenty of medicines but as often occurs on medical trips, all bags did not arrive. This is not the only country where our medicines and ministry items seem to be "lost" at a border crossing or in the luggage transfer at an airport. Sometimes, we can argue them back into existence. Often we just have to move on to Plan B. On our first medical trip into El Salvador, customs held our medicines and sent us directly to Plan B ... work with what you have and see what you can find within the country.

That first trip in 2000 was just the beginning of almost annual trips. Leadership training and medical clinics were accompanied by armed police escorts who never left any of us on our own. Violence and the threat of it were never far from our thoughts. But the spiritual rewards were great and our faith prevailed.

We were able to successfully complete four clinics our first week with make-shift huts of bamboo or tarps stretched over tree limbs to protect us from the sun. The medical team worked through heat and dust. We were blessed to have the assistance of other organizations including Operation Blessing and even a dentist from the 700 Club.

Memorable moments...El Salvador does have some of our best "missions stories". Having a small lady dentist from the area with us on one trip meant abscessed teeth coming out of old and young alike without a whimper – and without numbing medications! There is nothing like a dental clinic out under a stretched blue tarp on a bright summer day in the tropics.

We have worked in tents, churches and local schools over the years. On one occasion, a patient left the clinic only to return a half hour later to ask us to send medications and someone to a house nearby where a man was dying. The team that went ministered to the family and gave what advice and assistance they could, but it was clearly a terminal situation. Having provided medications and prayer, the team members left with heavy hearts. It was but a few minutes before a young child from the house came running to the clinic to give us a sack of fruit from their backyard tree – an offering of thanks.

It was on that same trip that Allen faced a seemingly disastrous blow. With such a large group, it is critical to have cash on hand, but he guards it closely and keeps it safely hidden. When he reached for the money to purchase needed clinic items, the money pouch was gone. Somehow it had been lost or stolen though pinned under his shirt. Missions work is often draining and stressful, and Satan loses no chance to push people deeper into the mud of despair. Allen was devastated as he sat in a corner with head low and then walked outside and stood in the pouring rain, trying to gather his spirit back. The money was never found, but spiritual deliverance into peace was forthcoming as the team lifted him up in prayer. And the mission team members, who had paid their way to get there, gave an offering to replace the loss. Finance is so critical to a ministry among those who have so little, but nothing is more vital than the love of God and His people.

And as every difficult time is matched with a victory, every set back eventually brings us to unexpected service. It was in El Salvador, in a school-yard clinic, that we encountered a lady of 80+ years. She approached the clinic doctor holding her arm stiffly. The arm had been broken a week before. It was not properly set and would require a re-breaking of the week's healing so it could be set properly. So what do you do in the middle of a rural school yard with no anesthesia and limited surgical supplies? Our doctor began to inspect the damaged arm, and the rest of the team went into action. Allen was blessed with "field ingenuity". He rushed to an area behind the buildings looking for a fairly large bamboo. Cutting it into a short strong piece and clearing it into a trough, it became a removable cast. Our youngest team member (age 15) saw the need and yanked out his brand new white T-shirt to tear into strips for a sling. The lady murmured not at all as they broke the bone where it had originally separated. Re-aligning the bones and wrapping it tightly, the doctor set it gently in the bamboo and tied the white t-shirt sling.

Most of those present remember the day well and still talk of it. But the report we received several years later nourished our spiritual hearts. The local pastor reported that the aged lady had accepted Jesus as Savior after we left and was a regular attender of his church. Things don't always follow our plans on the mission field, but God is always sufficient to provide a way to get the job done. He does indeed do more than we can "think or ask".

A later trip presented entirely different challenges. El Salvador is considered a very dangerous country because of gang activity, and MS-13 ranks as one of the largest, most violent gangs in the Americas. Their organization runs from Washington, D. C., to Boston, to Los Angeles, to their home territory in San Salvador. And we sat our medical clinic right in the middle of their territory. We did not realize how serious our situation was. The week before, gang members had shot a 12-year old in the leg for disobeying them. Then, because he was suffering so much and no medical help was available, they ended his suffering with a shot to the head. The gang ruled here. They made the rules, and we were working on their turf!

Clinic work went on as usual, interviewing, diagnosing, and distributing medicines. We felt no threat or fear but were aware that the young men in baggy pants, sleeveless shirts, and "the haircut" were checking us out. Rather than challenging or threatening us, they made favorable comments about the good we were doing for their people. My son, Allen, was able to talk with several of them during the day, witnessing to them about Christ and praying with some.

It was early afternoon, when several young men approached carrying an unconscious woman toward our building. She was barely alive. Our doctor laid her in the floor with feet elevated and sat in the floor beside her, constantly monitoring her vital signs. She was at the point of death. A call was made for an ambulance, but they refused to come into the area. A second ambulance company was called. "No," they would not enter the gang ruled area. A call for police assistance to get the woman to a hospital gave the same result. "We don't go there," was their response. After 20-30 minutes and several calls, an ambulance was located that agreed to come only if someone would meet them at the main highway to "escort" them in an out. A local church leader agreed, and the woman was finally transported to a hospital for critical care. It was a stressful day but basically "just another day of medical clinic."

My first trip to El Salvador did not come as soon as I desired, but our experiences in the country since then have been incredible, miraculous, and even enjoyable -- always expecting the unexpected. We have been able to return almost yearly with medical clinics and leadership training for a church in need. The church has multiplied by raising up new congregations. Several pastors from the United States have traveled with me and my son, Allen, to conduct training seminars, to help build new churches. There is great need to lift up the believers of El Salvador and energize them to "Go into all the World and make disciples".

ENGLAND and Wales

"You did not let that which hurt you stop you from your purpose" ...*ICM student*

From 1982 through 1987, Louise and I spent 3-6 months of every year directing the Center for International Christian Ministries (CICM). After that, I traveled back to England as a lecturer each fall. London became almost as familiar to me as Atlanta. I can drive on the left side of the road, eat fish and chips from a newspaper packet, and survive steak and kidney pie.

Our school was housed in a former hotel building that was 106 years old, relatively young by European standards. We occupied the three stories and had a basement for storage. First floor was classroom, kitchen, dining and office. Second floor was a dormitory for our 16 to 20 students. Up top, we had our personal "flat". Daily exercise was no concern as this was a true "walk up". Of course, it got easier as the old building sank an inch a year ...five years, five inches.

Term length was first set at six months but was later shortened to three months. Our students represented the top church leadership in their home countries, and such a long absence was detrimental to the home churches. They wanted more training but their responsibilities at home also weighed heavily on them.

Classes began at 8:30 in the morning, then a break at 10:00 for tea. Lunch break allowed a small amount of private time and food before afternoon classes from 2:00 until 4:00 sessions. My class, "Cross Cultural

Communications" was always first every morning. With students from at least five or six different countries, this was our most difficult and most valuable course. One memorable session included men from Nigeria, the Philippines, Hong Kong, Indonesia and South America. Many had never traveled outside their geographic areas. London, a very large city so far from home, was more than a little intimidating. We reserved weekends for a bit of rest and recreational education with trips into the English countryside and the visiting of historical landmarks.

Our students did not walk in the door as a cohesive group with similar backgrounds and expectations. They differed in their cultural experiences, their mannerisms their ideas of politeness, their daily work habits, and their approach to study. All came to the Center as leaders. They were accustomed to being in charge and directing activities, not to everyone else being on their same level or to anyone else being in charge. They were not arrogant. They were simply strong and competent personalities. So my task was to teach them flexibility and tolerance in behavior as much as to guide them in spiritual truth.

Other classes were presented by guest professionals who came in for two-weeks. Each had his or her area of specialty, instructing in such subjects as church leadership and management. The classes presented new ideas for the men and led to lively discussion as to how the principles taught could work effectively in their home settings. The principles gave a standard for all church groups and seldom changed. However, application at the local level often varied and offered fertile ground for discussion.

The melding of several different cultures as well as the newness of leaders becoming students led to some difficult times of adjustment.

THE CHALLENGE:

- *ARRIVAL:* Young man from Hong Kong arrived "knowing it all."
- *QUESTIONING ME:* What qualifications do you have to teach this course?
- *MY ANSWER:* A lifetime of experience. Is that enough?

TOILET DUTY: The tasks of dorm cleaning rotated among the students but "toilet cleaning" fell well beneath the dignity of one of our Chinese students.

- *REFUSAL:* The young man refused to take his turn and insisted I would just have to ask one of the other students to do it as he did not do such work.
- *MY RESPONSE:* "I cannot ask others. If you can't do it, I will have to do it."
- *HIS RESPONSE:* "But you can't do it. You're the President of the college."
- *MY REPLY:* "If you don't, I will have to do it."
- *THE RESULT:* A moment of silence and thought followed by a nod of the head and "I'll do it."

The experience changed the young man's attitude about the call to service. Today he is head of a church of 25,000 on the second floor of an eight floor building. He is nothing less than "dynamic" as a leader. He knows how to serve as well as how to lead.

Louise spent her days with much less interesting tasks such as grocery shopping, cooking, and washing sheets and towels. Cooking was her major chore but Louise is always equal to that challenge. She soon adapted her menus to include different foods from different cultures every evening. She even added the American tradition of a birthday cake on each man's special day. It was a new celebration to many and a personal recognition for them. Eventually, the men moved to "their night" in the kitchen where, with Louise's help, they produced their favorite meal for the group. However, none produced the all-time favorite. Louise's Southern fried chicken always hit the top of the favorite foods chart.

> **Lines from Louise ... in the kitchen**
> Our new student from India was just not doing well. Homesick! Depression set in with the move to unfamiliar housing, people who were strangers, and no Indian faces to share the news of home. Nothing was familiar. He spoke good English, but his heart spoke Telagu.
> "What would make you smile?" I asked.
> "Dahl ... Auntie could cook Dahl. I miss that most."
> Out came my Betty Crocker International cook book. Then out came my down coat, my rain boots, and my umbrella for a walk to the market. At dinner, he showered us all with smiles and "thank you's". A proper pot of lentil beans made all the difference.

Students learned from lectures but they were constantly watching Louise and me, aware of our personal attitude and actions. I used to suffer from nose bleeds ... intense nose bleeds. But for 19 years, I had been free of them. Free of them until I began a class on "Spiritual Warfare" at the Center. For the entire two weeks, I taught with a box of tissue beside me to control the bleeding. At the end of term, I asked the usual question, "What has impressed you most in your study here?" The response was quick. "It was your problem with your nose bleed, Rev. Skelton. You did not let that which hurt you stop you from your purpose. We have learned that we must always continue to our goal." I realized, as always, we teach more by example than by lecture.

Our former students are now scattered around the world leading Christian organizations and sharing what they learned in those London classes. Their commitment to the training was to share it with a minimum of 100 persons upon their return home. Our yearly sessions to some 20 students would reach 2000 students scattered over the globe. What seemed a small effort guided evangelism across the globe.

In fact, our London curriculum set the foundation for a wider training program throughout Central and South America. Fellow missionary and friend, June Carter, translated our CICM teaching materials into Spanish. As a team, we used our summers to teach the CURSOM program, an advanced leadership training. We taught in five different Spanish-speaking countries and over 35 churches during those early days. Currently, the program operates in over 19 Bible Colleges and 50 churches.

The London experience enriched our lives in other ways. At the end of each session, friends often came from the states to help us close the term and to take a short trip with us. Being so close to Europe, we could take easy and cheap bus or train travel. A few hundred dollars would get us to France, Switzerland, a tour of eight European nations, and even to one of my favorite areas, Scandinavia. We concluded our annual London duty with enjoyable travel and a chance to learn again of cultural difference.

WALES: The friendships I make in my ministry and travels are amazing. I still communicate frequently with the church leadership there. Wales is a wonderful place but not as well-known as other parts of the British Isles. To some, it is the east part of England. To others, it is the country separated from Ireland by a narrow sea channel. To many, it is a sovereign nation with its own language. Actually, Wales is all of the above.

Centuries ago, Wales lost its independent country status to become a sovereign state within the British Empire. However, most people recognize the crossing into Wales only because it is written on a road sign. Stay on any major Welsh road for long, and you will find yourself in England proper. Head toward the coast and you will find a quick ferry to Ireland. The country is bilingual with Welsh and English as official languages. British by law and government, the people never forget that they possess their unique Celtic culture and their distinctive history. They are Welsh.

From our educational ministry in London, the drive to Wales was about a five hour drive, convenient and a natural expansion of our ministry. The people of Wales extended great kindness and courtesy to Louise and my. We stayed with a local family that made us feel totally at home. We made the trip each year from London to teach advanced church leadership and other topics of interest to a gathering of the Welsh pastors. My first sermon there was "CHURCH ON FIRE ... BURNING WITH A MISSION." The following week was a teaching series on "Dynamic Biblical Leadership". Over 40 participants from a variety of churches and denominations attended. I was impressed with the openness of the people but also well aware that I stood on Holy Ground for Wales was the home of one of the world's greatest revivals in centuries past.

For our teaching session, the day ministry belonged to Louise while I spoke at the evening sessions. She taught on a different subject every day. "How to Get More Out of Your Bible" focused on daily Bible study. She encouraged a movement in Wales toward home prayer fellowships and discussed how to make them more effective. All of this was well received by the congregations. Wales is a nation of evangelism where prayer groups walk the streets claiming neighborhoods, villages and cities for God. They do not limit themselves to a church interior to spread the Gospel.

Churches in Wales have shown a steady progress, and in 2016, a new building was purchased to establish a training center modeled on the London school. As soon as renovations are made, Wales will have its own center of training and evangelism reaching out to the uttermost parts of the world.

The historical significance of the Welsh Revival of the early 1900's cannot be overlooked. A minister named Rev. Evan Roberts set the country of Wales on fire ... spiritually. Those flaming revival fires settled into a firm foundation of glowing embers that do not burn out. They hold the treasures of past history while providing fuel for revival in our generation. Wales was and is the center of one of the greatest revivals of modern times. The 1904 revival began in small churches throughout the Welsh countryside and eventually spread to Scandinavian, European and even Asian countries. The revival was a break from the formality common to British church services to an evangelistic Pentecostal outpouring. Literature of the day tells of entire communities where people were saved and turned from drunkenness and sin to upstanding citizenship and commitment to Holy living. It was the revival that greatly influenced the Azusa Street Revival of Los Angeles. And, of course, the Azusa Street Revival laid the foundation for Pentecostalism in the United States.

I visited the home of Evan Roberts on several occasions. It was well kept, and open only to tours in restricted areas. But, one day, I got my special blessing. There was no one at the home other than the caretaker. I spent several unforgettable hours walking through living quarters of the great evangelist, being allowed to sit in his study, browsing through his collection of books. Being in such a place of historical revival flooded my thoughts and emotions with humility. I knew I owed my present day ministry to God's miracles in ages past. Rev. Evan

Roberts set a foundation and a path for my ministry. My personal spiritual history is based in that Welsh revival,

The "Great Awakening" of the early 1900's burned brightly for some years and spread its evangelistic fire across countries and even across oceans. Those flames produced a foundation of life-giving embers to the evangelical church -- embers that continue to warm the evangelistic zeal of the Welsh. My spirit was warmed by that glow, and it burns brightly in my most pleasant memories.

GUATEMALA

"Utz Utz Pin Pin" (K'iche)

Land of contrast ... land of delight. Guatemala is incredibly beautiful and shows a broader range of culture and people than almost any country in Central America. But, for me personally, it had a bad introduction. My planned trip was not to Guatemala but through it. I was helping two new missionaries get to their station in Costa Rica, so we were driving the long road from McAllen, Texas, to San Jose, Costa Rica. At the entry to Guatemala, a well-armed border guard denied us entry. For six hours I "discussed" our entry with the guard. For six hours, he refused our passage. Then, for the umpteenth time, I insisted on talking with the official in charge and was finally directed to the door of the office building.

"What is your problem?" asked the man in charge.

"Sir, I've been sitting on your border for six hours with a couple on their way to Costa Rica. Your men have not given me permission to enter Guatemala. And, to be truthful, I cannot think of a single good thing to say about Guatemala when I return to the United States."

The official looked thoughtful for a moment, somewhere between anger and disgust, and then stood and motioned for me to follow. "Come with me," he said. Within minutes we were at the border crossing laying out our permits for the crossing. All I had needed was the "jefe", the boss. We were on our way, but we would not travel alone. Guatemala was in the midst of revolution, so an armed soldier was put in our car for the ride to the exit border. Driving quickly away after having wasted almost an entire day with the border crossing, we determined to spend no more than one night in Guatemala. Taking the first hotel we could find, we were oblivious to the proverbial "red light" known to everyone but us. The shutterless windows stood full open to the outside. We took turns staying awake for guard duty. That first impression of the country was not good – but first impressions can be wrong and in this case they were. Guatemala was to become one of my real favorites.

Our first church mission in Guatemala opened in 1978 in the mountain city of Quezaltenango. That first trip to organize the church was one crisis after another. A Baptist minister and I flew to Mexico City and then into Guatemala City. It was at the Mexican airport that my fellow traveler discovered he had left his passport at home. Not a good thing! It was one of those times when I just grab whatever comes into my head and say a prayer for help. As we neared the customs desks, I told my friend "stand as close to me as you can get." We approached the customs desk almost as one person. Stamp, stamp on my papers and passport and a wave through for the both of us. It was unbelievable. Still, I knew the Guatemalan entry would be even more difficult. Again, we moved as one through the customs line. Again, my friend was not noticed. My fellow minister had just managed to cross two international borders without a passport. A miracle? I think so.

From Guatemala City, we took the bus up into the mountains to Xela (Quezaltenango) to set in order the new missions outreach. Prior contacts with other missionaries helped us locate the congregation that sought to join our organization. Several days were spent conferencing with the local leadership and setting up procedures. Nothing more was needed than to get an early morning start on our long bus ride back to the Guatemala City and the airport.

We arose early and in darkness walked a mile or so to the bus station. As we neared the bus stop, our attention was drawn through the night to a pair of tail lights moving away from us. Our bus had left 30 minutes early. We trudged back to the city park totally disheartened. We had a plane to catch and needed to be on time. A conversation with some men in the park indicated there a bus leaving from the upper area of the park immediately. Two, not so young men, began to rush to the bus dragging our suitcases. We managed to capture the last two empty seats. Settling on the bus with a thankful heart, my friend asked, "Don't you live on the edge of a crisis?" "No," I replied. "I live on the edge of a miracle." Our second-choice bus was faster than our original reservation, and we arrived in Guatemala City 30 minutes before the other one. When things seem to go against you, wait for the Lord to provide a better option. Look for the "miracle".

By 2002, the Guatemalan organization had grown to 90 churches and missions. The largest church seated 1500 people. We traveled back to the mountains to conduct leadership seminars with local workers. One of my greatest missions memories is a service in a church built in honor of Clifford Skelton, my father. He was not only a great father but also a great mission supporter who raised two children to be missionaries. My son Allen, and I did a "tag team" on Sunday night with Allen's sermon on

"Opportunity" and my following it with the same topic. The people were spiritually moved. And, we both gave thanks for the heritage left us by my father.

But sometimes, our services took great effort. A few nights later, we hiked through a corn field to speak in a church with 308 members. The congregation spoke only a Mayan dialect and wore traditional Mayan clothing. It was a wonderful service but such language barriers tire the speakers greatly. It was the love of the people and their response to our ministry that made even the difficulty of getting there seem as nothing.

> ### *Lines from Louise Skelton* ~~
> *My most memorable trip to Coatepeque, Guatemala, was one where we lived out of our suitcases in tiny hotel rooms. It was two and a half hours more go to an area outside of Quezaltenango on Sunday. We sighed and began walking the path through a recent flood area. Past a washed out bridge and over a make-shift foot bridge, we thought we had arrived exactly in time for the 3 o'clock service. But, the service was a 2 o'clock service ... ooops! We were late... but not to worry. It had been a special day of celebration for a young girl's "quinceanera", one of the most wonderful birthdays of her life, number 15. As is the custom, it was being celebrated with a special ceremony, gifts and a gathering of almost the entire community. So we enjoyed the festivities and the joy of the family before we entered into a service of ministry and music. It turned out to be a day of great worship as well as great photographs.*

Besides evangelistic church work, we visit the country with several medical missions every year. In Guatemala, the teams have worked mostly out of the colonial city of Antigua. Vicky Skelton, my daughter-in-law, sets them up in cooperation with local churches and leaders, and these trips are a favorite with many of our team members. We spend most of the Guatemalan clinics in various Mayan villages. Everyone has to be up, finished with breakfast, and loaded into the vans or bus by 8 am. Somewhere in there, suitcases and boxes of medications and supplies have to be strapped to the top of the vehicles. The norm is several hours of traveling along rough mountain roads, dodging rock and mud slides or passing through water filled gullies in the roadway. We know we have arrived when we see the lines of people waiting for our clinic. They never fail to treat us kindly, bringing what gifts they have of home grown foods and fruits. We, in turn, empty our suitcases of medicines, hand out our gifts for the children, and preach the Gospel of Jesus Christ.

The language factor in Guatemala is a challenge as well as a unique joy. The country has over nineteen ethnic groups and forty-nine languages. While Spanish is the major language, many mountain villages speak only a native Mayan dialect. Our trips to outlying villages are filled with people discussing their physical need with medical professionals or trying on reading glasses. "Utz Utz Pin Pin" is often heard in some areas. It is a phrase in K'iche meaning "very good". It seemed to be their favorite phrase, or maybe it was the only phrase we came to understand in the local Mayan dialect. From south to north, the Mayan groups still have their territories.

Languages such as Kaqchikel and K'iche are common. In the village of La Cumbre, 90% or more of the people spoke only K'iche, no Spanish.

> Clinic work went like this:
> 1-Eng: "When did this problem begin?"
> 2-Sp:"Cuando comenzo este problema?"
> 3-Sp. to K'iche "………………?"
> 4-K'iche response: "………………."
> 5-K'iche to Sp. ." Casi dos meses."
> 6-Sp. to Eng. "About 2 months."

Every communication went through six language steps and involved four persons – our medical team professional, an interpreter from English to Spanish, an interpreter form Spanish to K'iche, a K'iche speaking client, and then back through the group to the doctor/nurse.

Fortunately, I was blessed to have fine help in spiritual clinic and was able to go from Spanish to K'iche and back, skipping the English all together. The day was long but successful in an area in need of the most basic of medical supplies and treatment. Our bus ride back to the hotel was unusually quiet as mental exhaustion took over. We were tired but the week had been overwhelmingly successful with 1500 sick treated, 290 pairs of reading glasses given out, food supplied for 500 families, and toys and clothes to the children. Over 180 confessed faith in Jesus as Savior.

But at the end of our work day, the land of contrast shows her other side. The city of Antigua gives us rest. This colonial city, originally the capital of Guatemala, is a "walking town". The rough cobblestone streets require careful steps or the hire of a "tuk tuk" for travel. This "tuk tuk" is actually a motorcycle converted into a three-wheel vehicle of sorts with a canvas covered frame with room for two or three passengers. There is no Cadillac comfort on the harsh stone streets, but the transport is fast, and dry, and even fun.

Five volcanoes in various stages of eruption surround the city leaving one always searching their peaks for black puffs of smoke. A heavy rainy season produces mudslides and puddles to walk through. And yet, it is a place of beauty and charm like no place else. After a hard day of clinic, everyone looks forward to rest at a charming local hotel, walking along ancient streets with indigenous women in Mayan dress, a nice dinner "on the mountain", or being sure to order your "flan" at the beginning of your evening meal lest others get it all before you.

Besides frequent travel to the city of Antigua, we have also traveled to the southern Mayan highlands in the "state" of Chiquimula. Some in our medical team insist that we had gone to the "uttermost part of the earth" when we finally arrived in Camotan, Guatemala. One trip had our group traveling from Guatemala City down toward the border with Honduras on an old yellow school bus. You can imagine the comfort of traveling for 6 hours on those unpadded seats with no air conditioning.

In missions work of all kinds, we often join with other established evangelical groups. Our goals are cooperative rather than competitive, and there is plenty of work to be done. On this trip, we were hosted for the week by a local missionary who had established a ministry among the surrounding mountain villages. The local ministry included preaching and teaching but also a program of assistance to the economically depressed area. Our team lived dorm style and climbed onto trucks every morning for an hour or more of "stand up" travel. Four pick-up trucks transported us over rough and rugged roads, through creek beds, and up mountains. It was an area of the Chorti tribe with few resources and sparse education. People often walked two miles just to get to a bus to get to school or any sort of store. We conducted four days of clinic, either in the mountain villages or in the building on the compound where we stayed. It was not a trip of fun and games, but then our goal is not to be "tourists'. Our goal is to meet the needs of the people.

But, some adventurous team members seem to always find time for something different. I must say I missed the 20 team members in the back of small pick-up truck going through the dark to the natural hot water springs. I also have been told that it was better to go there at night as the place looked better in the dark than the light. Still, everyone came back safe with a story to tell.

The trip to Camotan, the harsh travel, and the struggle to communicate was a bit "out of our comfort zones" but such struggles totally pale in light of being a part of an exciting adventure for the Kingdom of God. Why do we go? This trip, 1700+ patients received medical care. At least 365 received reading glasses. And new souls added to the Kingdom were over 170.

"This baby is dying as I hold it in my arms."~~~~
It happened in Camotan and the words came from our primary physician for medical missions. The baby in the doctor's arms was indeed lifeless, seemingly comatose. The anxious mother watched as two of her other youngsters played around her, and another reached for her breast to nurse. The infant was in a state of total malnutrition seeking milk from a mother who had no milk to give. Formula in a bottle was the obvious answer, but such was just not available or even well understood in the mountain area. And, how about a hospital for this child for immediate care? No, the mother could not go there. She had her other children to care for, and the hospital required someone to stay in attendance with the child at all times. Even if the money for a hospital could be collected, there was no one who could go with the child. We watched helplessly as the gaunt mother continually tried to give the comatose child a dry nipple to suck. Local missionaries searched for answers, but there were none. The mother gathered her children and started for home. We sent formula and tried to give the mother directions for feeding, but she continued to guide the child to her empty breast for milk. Our only solution was to pray ... pray for a miracle of care, a miracle of strength, a miracle of wisdom. It was a scene we would never lose from our minds ... never.

- Brazil service
- Chilean street
- Preacher at work

- Spiritual clinic
- Louise with baby
- Waiting for clinic

- Counseling
- Delivering food boxes
- Planning the next step

GUYANA

"Timing is everything"

On the northeast coast of South America, there are three small countries. Guyana is the most northern, bordering Brazil and close to the islands of Trinidad and Tobago in the Caribbean. It is a country known to few travelers but to many mosquitos. In the hotel lobby, in the restaurants, in the streets, in bed, we swatted at mosquitos. They loved us. This is a land of dirt roads, of bicycles rather than cars, and of old dilapidated buildings. Because of its closeness to the Caribbean islands historically and culturally, it is considered to be more Caribbean than South American in style. Guyana is an unexplored area of forest and jungle, giving it a unique place in environmental study. The country is not on the "tourist track" for many, but it retains one of the largest animal and plant biospheres in the world. Visitors are more likely to be scientists than tourists.

Being in God's time is critical to success in the ministry and in any spiritual endeavor. Our first trip to Guyana, South America, was definitely in proper time. My son Allen and I, visit Brazil almost every year in early December. We speak at two large conferences in the city of Fortaleza, Brazil, and we visit a number of churches. On one such visit, it was suggested that we make a trip into Guyana to see about establishing church work there. Of course, we were ready for any new adventure. We hopped on a small plane and headed to a land where the people looked and spoke more like the people of Tobago and Trinidad than of its neighbor Brazil.

Life as a colony under British rule until 1966 left Guyana with English as its official language and a rather British legal system. In the capital of Georgetown, it is obvious that the old one-story buildings have been treated with care, but they sag toward the decay of age. Only one building attracts immediate attention. Standing in the center of town is an unforgettable structure built many years ago by the Church of England. It would be an unusual and fascinating structure anywhere. But among the decay of Georgetown, it is truly magnificent ... one of the most interesting buildings I have ever seen. Like an oasis in a desert, the multi-level church radiates beauty, seeming to soar above the single-level sagging buildings more common to the area.

Upon arrival in the capital city we were given a tour and daily transportation courtesy of a local businessman. A Brazilian pastor had traveled with us and introduced us to two business women of the city who had been holding regular church services and were ready to set the church in order officially. Their congregation had grown to the point that they felt a need to establish a clear governing body to oversee the church growth. They had done a good work in the city, but it was time to expand and for that, some guidance and support was needed.

After a few days of prayer and discussion with the ladies, it was agreed that the positions of Pastor and Assistant Pastor should be divided between the two of them. As they carried the daily responsibility of the evangelistic work, an experienced pastor from the nearby city of Boa Vista, Brazil, would provide them with counsel and guidance. He agreed to travel to the Georgetown area twice monthly to assist these local pastors. Once again, I was delighted to see how missions work in the field is a cooperative endeavor. The focus is on the work of the church and the needs of the congregation with little concern for difference of nationality or even language.

This same cooperative action followed us to our next stop, the city of Lethem, Guyana. A small plane which seated only 12 persons took us on a 2 ½ hour flight toward the Brazilian border further into the jungle. Allen was about the only one of us who enjoyed the plane. He spent our return flight mesmerized by the pilot's work. Having a full load, Allen was seated in the co-pilot seat and used the flight to strengthen his own pilot training. We planned church work while Allen talked aeronautics with our pilot.

The plane landed safely in Lethem on their single runway, and we strolled past the one bench that made up the airport waiting area. The city itself is completely new. Because there are no roads of length in Guyana and the people of the area are so isolated from the rest of the country, the government determined to "plant" a city in the southern area to supply the needs of those living there. The city itself has been cut out of the dense jungle. Government buildings stand in stark contrast to the surrounding almost impassable foliage.

In Lethem, we met with the church workers to discuss their needs for organization and support. One day, they took us out of town to visit a Momo Indian village of over a thousand people. Clearly, the people of the village had never seen luxury. It was not an area of hot water, inside bathrooms, or flat screen TV's. The homes were little more than huts made with whatever could be found. Mud was the major construction material with scraps of salvaged tin or board interspersed. Roofs were thatched with nearby grasses and jungle plants. There was no "building code" or plan evident. People put up one or two huts as they preferred for their families. Doorways usually numbered one per building though some splurged for two. Maybe the hut would have a single window cut into the wall with a piece of wooden shutter to close at night. A few spoke Portuguese or a little Spanish but most kept to their local dialect. And despite our "foreignness" in speech and looks, the people extended immediate hands of friendship. I well remember the elderly lady who declared to me that she was 100 years old. I had no proof of her claim, but I know she sure looked 100 or even more.

Back in Lethem, we met to set the local church in order. A local ministerial worker was assigned the dual task of leading the local church services and of maintaining a close contact with the ladies of Georgetown and their work. Then, the more experienced pastor from just across the Brazilian border in Boa Vista would become mentor to the Lethem church minister and his congregation. It was an agreeable plan, a very workable one as it turned out. Since those initial visits, the churches in both major cities of Guyana have grown in number and in outreach to the community. Administrative church officials from the United States have since made several trips to encourage the churches. It was a blessing to visit and help establish a true "kingdom connection" with these wonderful people.

HAITI

"For I was hungred and you fed me ... I was a stranger and you took me in." (Matt. 25:35)

The first day was very interesting. The second day was incredible. The third was miraculous. We arrived in Haiti to feed the hungry, minister the Gospel, and even offer medical support for the wounded. A major earthquake had left the villages of small huts flattened. The people waded through mud and feared to go inside any type of construction. Water ran in the dirt roads but not in any houses or faucets for drinking. We were not mentally or emotionally prepared for the destruction we saw, but then the Haitian people were not prepared for what they were enduring.

That first day was "interesting" as I saw Haiti for the first time and realized the poverty that enveloped the country. The second day was "incredible" as we began feeding the people and ministering to them. The third day was "miraculous" when we found a dying child abandoned under a missions compound.

We settled into our living area as quickly as possible and rushed to the feeding area to deliver hot meals to injured people lying on cots in tents. Some had lost a limb. Others suffered open wounds and injuries. Hundreds had lost all their possessions in the quake. Homes, furnishings, clothes, and personal belongings were all gone. Even worse was the loss of family members.

Many children had lost one or both parents and were in the care of relatives. Some were taken in by total strangers. One lady struggled to recover from her eight day ordeal under the rubble of the Catholic Church. It was staggering to see and to listen to the tragic stories. But we had work to do greater than listening.

Thirty-nine trucks were lined up and loaded with food in a cooperative effort with "Love a Child Ministries". The food distribution would save thousands of lives. Beginning in the city, we gradually moved farther out into the mountains where the need was even greater. Day after day, we took food to village after village ... sometimes riding the trucks, sometimes leaving the trucks behind and carrying food as we walked where there were no roads to drive on. One day, we had to hike up a river bed to a high mountain village. Another trip took our trucks down a dry river bed. Our convoy climbed through holes and dodged boulders. When we came to an intensely steep incline, our driver knew she could not handle the situation. A more experienced driver from another truck in the convoy was asked to come and take us down. He took it slow and had no major problem. Those of us riding in the truck had lots of problems. We held our breath and prayed. Once back to "terrible road" instead of "impossible road", our own driver took the wheel again. The other driver had to go back to his truck and do it all over again.

At the mountain mission station, we found several hundred women and children waiting to get food. First on the agenda was to cook for the children. A basic meal was served to them. Their hunger was evident. And there were signs that malnutrition and even starvation had set in for some. The clue was in their hair color. A reddish tint to the hair was a clear sign that starvation was setting in.

Each child ate quietly, dipping fingers into the plastic bowls politely but leaving no scraps of uneaten food. We then began the task of distributing food for the families. The women lined up behind the trucks and waited patiently. One of our team members checked off each woman's identity card while I lifted a 33 lb. box of rice, beans and other staples off the truck and onto her head. With perfect balance, each lady gathered her children and began her journey back home. One lady had walked for two hours just to get there. And, she would walk two more hours back with a heavy box on her head. We gave out over 200 boxes of food that day.

The days in Haiti had no planned variety. It was a matter of getting up and doing whatever needed to be done in that place on that day. Evenings brought us exhaustion from the work and from the emotional stress of seeing so much suffering. We conducted evening church services in several missions and villages. The orphanage was used to set up food distribution as well as for our services.

As the week progressed, I began to hear of a "voodoo priest" who had become a Gospel evangelist. I set out to find him in the tent city, wanting to hear his story. He said he had become a voodoo priest early in life. Every day he had worn a snake wrapped around his neck and considered the snake to be his source of power. When he wanted to help the people or do something miraculous, he would ask the snake to help him. And, of courses, he asked the snake to protect him from harm. But as the earthquake took its toll, he found himself unable to help the people. His snake was of no use. He asked the snake for help but the power was not there. The snake could do nothing to bring help. As he watched the suffering around him, the man remembered having heard a minister who talked of "Jesus" and the power of Jesus to help people. The Voodoo priest began to search and to enquire, "Where is the man who talks of the man named Jesus?" He found the minister and listened to the Gospel message. Turning his heart to Jesus, the voodoo priest abandoned his former life. He took off his snake and destroyed it. He took on the spirit of Jesus and began a true ministry. He found in the Gospel the power to help people through prayer and preaching. I personally, know the power of the Lord in all things but am still amazed and delighted at His work in the lives of those who are open to Him. The man's testimony poured strength into my spirit.

My own sermon on the last night of our trip made me aware that the people of Haiti are starving spiritually as well as physically. They live on a "half island", sharing its small land mass with the Dominican Republic. The ocean breezes and years of stability have brought the Dominican a bounty of good agriculture and a booming tourist economy. But the Haitian side of the island crowds over 10 million people into a third part of the island. The people seek to survive in diversity ... diversity of cultures, diversity of languages, tribal conflicts, and economic bleakness. It is an impoverished nation with neither ability nor education to move forward. Bedeviled as they are by poverty both physically and spiritually, they are our spiritual brothers and sisters to whom we owe prayer and Christian charity.

Honduras

"Can a country be born in a day or a nation be brought forth in a moment?" (Is. 66:8 NIV)

In 2013, we saw it happen. July 13th saw the arrival of a fleet of 747 aircraft from Miami with thousands of Christians from 15 different states to evangelize every school possible in Honduras. An 18 container shipment arrived with 5 million meals, plus medical supplies and equipment. On July 20, missionaries congregated in the largest plazas and stadiums of each of the 18 states of Honduras to present the Gospel. During that week, medical brigades distributed millions of dollars of live-saving assistance. White Fields Mission participated at the stadium in La Ceiba, Honduras with 65,000 people in attendance. It was one of my many many trips to Honduras.

Probably more than any other country of the world, I have found myself in Honduras. Three major cities, Tegucigalpa, San Pedro Sula, La Ceiba, are like old friends. They just keep appearing out my airplane window. The country of Honduras keeps itself in the top three for poverty and for crime in the Western Hemisphere. It is a major distribution area for drug dealers and crime activity. Yet, I love going to Honduras. Why do I go so often and find it so inviting? Well, despite the problems, it is a beautiful country filled with kind and caring people. And, my son lives there.

Our only child, Allen, and his wife Vicky, moved to La Ceiba, Honduras in 2005 to establish White Fields ministry and to create a missions compound of accommodations and classrooms for missionary endeavor. I go there for international leadership conferences, for evangelism, and for medical clinics. But I must admit I get special joy in being with Allen and Vicky, working and planning with them, just encouraging one another in the work.

Tegucigalpa

The capital city of Honduras has over a million people. It is a city where we are blessed with good people to help in every phase of our ministry there. Whatever our goal or project, Christ for the Nations church will call on its membership to assist in the work. Nowhere do we get more competent help in our medical clinics than in "Teguc". Our friends there provide spiritual support, transportation assistance, and project management. Because of my long association with them, I approach my sessions of leadership training, church conferences, and teaching among them with absolute joy.

The medical clinics that Louise and I work in several times a year began in "Teguc". We marked the 100th clinic of the White Fields/ Omega ministry in the same city where the clinics began 12 years before. On the average, a clinic provides treatment for 1000-1500 patients in a week, reports 400 or more salvations, and gives out over 400 eye glasses. The 100th clinic was a time to celebrate, but it was really just a stepping stone to the 101st clinic.

From a small beginning, the local church has grown into a major influence in the city, giving rise to smaller church groups in the surrounding mountain area. Their emphasis is on the Christian ethics of witnessing and helping others. It is always a good thing to work among old friends. I enjoy most of my time in the busy city ... most of the time! But, there was one unfortunate departure that I don't like to remember.

After a week of hard work in medical clinic, team members boarded the plane for a direct flight to Atlanta, settled into their seats and hoped for a good nap on the way home. Unfortunately, Tegucigalpa airport is located in a deep valley among high mountains. When the strong winds prevent a good take off, the pilot simply asks a few folks to voluntarily take another flight. Our flight needed to be lighter by 35 people and all luggage on board. Our entire team thought it a good plan to take the "Delta deal". We would get a flight out the next day, a free night and meals at a top hotel, and a cash bonus. Sounded good ... but they failed to tell us that the flight we would get was actually leaving San Pedro Sula so we would go barreling through mountain roads in the dark to make a 157 mile trip by van.

We did get a nice hotel for the night. We did get delicious meals. We did get our bonus money. And, we did get home the next day. Was that trip on dark mountain curves with a speedy driver was worth it? I'm not sure. What I am sure of is that ministry in Tegucigalpa is exciting and worthwhile. The unusual departure did not deter me from my yearly trips to the capital of Honduras.

San Pedro Sula

The second largest city in Honduras is noted for its economic leadership...and for its violent crimes. Our choice of places to stay is the Grand Hotel Sula. Right in the middle of town, the hotel overlooks the crowded plaza and provides "people watching" from our hotel window. We have chosen to stay there almost every trip since 1963. We love to sit in the hotel and watch the city plaza with its crowd of local activities. We love to eat banana splits and everything else so wonderfully served in their restaurant. And, we love remembering our times in the city even before it was rated the "murder capital of the world".

Danger is a part of every country and every trip. But, fear is not. The Lord is faithful to keep us. It is not good to remember seeing a man shot to death on the street as we rode to the airport. It is not pleasant to remember the poverty that is clearly evident and the children wandering the streets without shelter or parenting. But, these memories are offset by visions of children who have been saved from a life that had no direction. I also see people who are finding a spiritual commitment to lighten their sorrows, people working together and caring for one another. San Pedro Sula is a city in need, but also a city with hope.

Our missions work in San Pedro Sula actually began in Choloma, a village about 12 miles out of the city. Our first church was built there over 50 years ago. An orphanage was also established to provide a home, access to education, and occupational training for boys from the street. The orphanage sits on the side of that same mountain today, working to give homeless children a new outlook on life and a vision for the future.

The church work in Choloma has prospered greatly and has spread its influence a bit farther out to the city of El Progreso. From the city churches, over 100 church sponsored cell groups have formed, meeting in homes to worship. Every Sunday, the founder of our work in the area directs five buses in their task to pick up church members and bring them into service.

A major task for me has been providing training for pastors and workers in the San Pedro Sula area. In more recent years, medical clinic trips take me there at least once a year. It is a beautiful city, but it is dangerous. Prayer is needed that our local ministers might be strengthened and organized to deal with troubling issues such as the rise in gang activity and the horrendous problem of street children. Drug lords rule the neighborhoods, and gang warfare is common. But our Lord rules over all, and His Word is sufficient to meet every difficulty, every challenge. We put our trust in Him.

Medical clinics and ministry outside our home country bring us challenges that are past counting. One trip to San Pedro Sula found us with no luggage for three days. We could survive the clothing problem, but our medicines and supplies were "lost in space" by the airline. Our clinics are intentionally located in poorer areas where the need is greater. One such area had only shacks made by leaning scraps of tin against each other. One church building had a floor, a roof and no walls. Another time, we were under spread tarps fighting excessive heat, crying babies, and barking dogs. But, always be thankful for what you have because there were times when just an area of shade trees had to suffice. Yet, I preached the Gospel while our clinic team saw the sick and gave out bags filled with rice, beans, corn meal, and cooking oil. We are propelled by the need, not ease or comfort.

It was in San Pedro Sula that I saw a totally unique event for our medical clinics. In 2002, we encountered patients in desperate need of surgeries which is a bit unusual. Such work is beyond a clinic set up under a tarp with crowds of onlookers. Eighteen patients needed surgery of some type so we set out on "Mission Impossible". We planned to ask the area hospital to let us use their facilities. I interpreted as one of our leaders sought permission. Refusal – it is not done! That was only the first rung of the ladder, so we started climbing that ladder of authority until we reached the Chief Executive of the hospital. After much thought, a glimmer of hope appeared. We could use the hospital facilities, and the local staff would assist our doctors. But, in return, we had to agree to assist and advise the local doctors as they operated on their patients. It would be a shared learning experience. Our doctors and the Honduran doctors formed a team. Never have I seen a foreign government give such cooperation and access as to open their medical facilities to us. The Lord opens doors that seem to be firmly shut.

The city of San Pedro Sula is filled with danger and violence. But, it is also occupied by strong, dedicated people who care about the city and its people. We are called to minister wherever there is need. Sometimes we are surprised to see the almost impossible happen. There is great need there, but there is also great potential. God's power and His people can make a difference.

La Ceiba

Our third city is, of course, La Ceiba, known as the tourist city of Honduras. The large Ceiba tree, valued by laborers for its inviting shade, gives the city its name. The port area allows cargo transit through the Caribbean as well as access to the sandy beaches of the Bay Islands. It is a city of beauty, but also has an abundance of heat, rain, bugs, ants, and mosquitos. I'm well acquainted with all of them.

My abilities are taxed to the limit in La Ceiba, but that is only because the opportunities are so varied. Our son, Allen, has taken a property just outside the city, two or three blocks from the ocean, and made it into his ministerial headquarters and a base for service. From the White Fields compound, you can teach English in the local school, hold Bible classes for the children of the community, or teach computer to some local teens. Or, you can get in the van and drive to help at the orphanage, visit the senior's home, or take a shovel and help rebuild a village. There is also opportunity to attend, work with, or speak to gatherings of the church leadership throughout Central America. And if you have a month or so, you can become an "intern" and help with all of the above activities while living on the property.

Where there was once one house and a smaller "cabin" for sleeping, there are now ten small cabanas complete with kitchen and bathrooms. They were built by donations and each bears the name of a Central American country. Louise and I always sleep in the Costa Rica house.

> **Lines from Louise...**
> As the plane taxied down the runway in Atlanta, tears coursed down my face...tears of gratitude, no less. It was my first trip since a heart attack in April of that year. Memories of past mission trips flooded my mind, but this one was to become **very special**. It was to be two weeks of teaching, training, and ministering to all ages. I would be once more "on the mission field" where I belonged.

It was in La Ceiba that Allen and Vicky inaugurated their first ministerial conference. Ministers and their wives gathered from all over Central America as well as Brazil and the United States. I taught leadership classes as usual, but even more valuable was time spent moderating discussions. The meetings gave pastors and leaders a place for sharing their problems, answers, victories and plans for the future. It has become an annual event, giving ministers and their wives a time of rest as well as a time of encouragement. We are called to minister to the needy but often forget that the workers in the vineyard of the Lord also need emotional and spiritual support.

And, White Fields has actually rebuilt an entire village. A large familial community had taken up residence in an isolated, overgrown field outside La Ceiba. Though they had been there for years with their mud and stick housing, the property owner decided to recoup his property and forced them out. The need led Allen and a fellow minister to find and fund a new place for them. Money was raised new land, and the entire village moved. They set up as usual with their houses of mud and stick. Kitchens were clay stoves built into the corner of the room and running water or plumbing was still non-existent.

I've done a lot of building over the years, but it was Allen's turn now. I got by with giving advice and helping to solve a few construction problems. Allen invested in a block making machine and trained men from the village to use it. The scene changed. That village now has over 28 block houses, a church/community center and a well system that has faucets located throughout the village. The children are now close enough to get to school on a bus. Visiting the village is always on my list when in La Ceiba. It will remain a "work in progress" because each step forward opens another opportunity to advance.

Of course, La Ceiba has also provided fertile ground for medical clinics. Louise and I attend at least one a year in the area, battling heat and humidity to deliver the Gospel story for souls as well as medicines for the sick.

"We must get this baby to a hospital. She is suffering from severe malnutrition and needs a blood transfusion immediately." The words came from the pastor's wife who knew what she was talking about. She was a licensed pediatrician. But the parents had no money for medical care. What could be done?

Gathering as a team, we prayed for the child, and then took an offering to send the family to the local hospital. Our medical team members are committed to helping others, but also to giving when needed. They bear the hearts of servants in the Lord's work.

It was in that same clinic that a lady had a stroke as she waited for medications in the clinic. Again, it was beyond our team's ability, but we were able to get her to a hospital.

I am reminded that since my youth, I have been on a continual rescue mission. Whether it be the soul that is in need or the person's body, my responsibilities are the same. I must "rescue the perishing…duty demands it." And, the country of Honduras is constantly calling.

INDIA

"Old friends and fried chicken".

It took me two years of red tape and delay to get to India. I finally arrived in Hyderabad about 2:40 in the morning for a two-week stay. A giant hug greeted me. A man I had not seen in 33 years or more was glad to see me. Bishop Moses Kumar had been a student at our Center for International Christian Ministries School in London. Now he was in charge of the all the Pentecostal Holiness Churches in his area of southern India. It was wonderful to see that this former student had grown into a powerful minister and now led an entire evangelistic association in India.

Getting to India was not easy. My application for a visa met barrier after barrier. After two years of phone calls and more money than it should have cost, I called my local congressman's office for help. The visa came within a week. I wish I had realized the value of political pressure earlier. But, the time and effort were worth it. I had come with some dear friends, missionaries who visit Hyderabad, India, almost every year to assist and help in the church work there. Our flight was long and seemingly difficult, but a stop in Dubai gave us time for a quick tourist look around. It provided a much needed break and a chance to see a new country and a new culture. That always makes a trip better for me.

Our hosts in Hyderabad rolled out the red carpet and treated us like royalty. Our rooms were on the grounds of the Bible College. I had a room and bath to myself with the blessing of both a fan and an air conditioner. Brother Moses has traveled widely and knows how to provide well for his guests. One of his daughters was in the U.S. studying at the time of our visit to India. Another had also studied in the States and had married an American. She and her husband then chose to live in Hyderabad and establish their ministry there. One of my finest memories of our trip was an invitation to lunch at their home. She set out a lunch of corn on the cob, mashed potatoes, and fried chicken. Her "southern cooking" made me think I had died and gone to heaven.

Adapting to Indian life style outside the compound took me a few days. I found the man on the street in Hyderabad to be much more aggressive than I was used to. They moved as a crowd, having to push and shove their way along. It was an "every man for himself" mentality, definitely resulting from the mass of population that is India. The traffic crowd was no less aggressive. Roads were filled with a mixture of cars, vans, buses, motorbikes, bicycles and even ox carts and seemed to reject any thought of driving courtesy or rules of safety.

Staying in the same compound with the church was indeed a blessing, an escape from noise and the press of humanity, an oasis of peace. This was really important because my schedule called for three sermons at the church as well as classes in Discipleship and Leadership for pastors and church leaders. The ministers and workers came in from different areas and stayed at the campus (school) for the entire conference.

I was also privileged to speak at the graduation ceremony for the college. I was honored to receive a "Life

Achievement Award" which cited my "manifold ministries to the global body of Christ for over seven decades." The award ceremony was done in true India style, complete with special dress and a traditional hat which I still have. Such public honor was embarrassing, wonderful, and humbling. All seemed to flood my heart at the same time.

In addition to working with Bishop Kumar at the conference, I took a day trip of 70 miles to the church compound and orphanage of the Congregational Holiness Church. Having survived the rush of overloaded trucks and no road rules, I was delighted with both my safe arrival and the extraordinary work that was being done there. The compound consisted of four acres in a small town setting, away from the hustle and bustle of the big city. The modern upscale buildings were home to over 120 children from ages 4 to 14 years. I was invited to speak to several of the classes that were in progress, and left feeling it was just "a really nice place." The ministry there provides hope and the possibility of a good future to children who have been left homeless on the streets. The social, emotional, and spiritual needs are all treated by the loving workers in the orphanage.

There is one other unforgettable moment of the trip, and it has nothing to do with orphanages. It was my Kentucky Fried Chicken moment! "How would you like some KFC for lunch today, Brother Hugh?" That was a symphony of music to a man like me who isn't truly fond of curry or casseroles.

Braving the city traffic, we settled ourselves into the crowded restaurant to eat. We were discussing the services and the missions efforts, not noticing that a man nearby was listening to all we said. The well-dressed man, speaking flawless English, came to our table and began asking about our visit in the city and our ministry. He kindly ordered us some free food and then asked if we would pray for him. Now? Right here in the middle of the lunch crowd? Yes? That's what he was asking. And, of course, we did as he asked. The man then revealed that he was actually the restaurant manager. He offered us a personal tour of the restaurant ... including the back kitchen. My mind was thinking, "If I visit the kitchen, I will probably never want to go into a KFC again in any country." I was wrong.

The place was amazing! I have never seen such a clean, shiny cooking establishment in my life. The place was spotless with electronic timers on the appliances and thermometers keeping watch over the food at all times. It drove home that old truth that says we cannot make assumptions about what we have not seen. We cannot judge by our past experiences. If we look, we can find the best of things in unlikely places.

Our host was rightfully proud of his business. He topped off our visit with a round of dessert bars. So for the second time, once in a home and now in a commercial restaurant, I experienced the delight of "southern fried chicken" in India.

But on the spiritual side, India is not so fresh and inviting. It remains one of the most difficult countries of the world for Christian ministry. The major religion is Hinduism which accepts many gods. Thus, it is easy to consider Jesus just another god to add to the list. India is also the home of over 172 million Muslims. More than

400 million have never heard the name of Jesus and over 500,000 villages have no Christian witnesses. It is the second most populated country in the world, plagued by massive poverty and overcrowded cities. Please pray daily for India and the fine people who spend their days spreading the Gospel among a needy people. Think of India as an exotic land of beauty, ancient history and culture. But always remember that it is a country of need materially and spiritually.

KENYA

"God's Resting Place"

My travel to Kenya, Africa, brought an answer to my prayer of 26 years to minister in that area. Sometimes, we have the right objectives, but we have to wait for God's timing. It was a special time for me, and it drove home the message that "God is faithful." He doesn't always work on our timetable or our plans, but He always answers our sincere prayers.

Though there is debate about it, most agree that the name "Kenya" evolved from tribal languages meaning "God's Resting Place." Whatever the case, it is also a country with need for God's work. It is one of the better known African countries among tourists, noted for the finest of safari game viewing. Few realize that the present Queen of England, Elizabeth II, actually ascended to the British throne while in Kenya. She and her husband were visiting the country when news of her father's death required an immediate return home to take the throne of England.

One thinks of the country on the Equator as a hot place. Yet, that is only the northern inland area. The Indian Ocean to southeast and Lake Victoria to the western border provide enough moisture and cool air to create a milder climate suitable for jungle growth and a large amount of wild life. Throw in a nice Mt. Kenya high enough to gather snow and you have a country of diversity attractive to everyone. I was fortunate to not only spend time ministering in Kenya, but also to travel to the border of Tanzania to speak for a service there.

However, the history of the country has slowed progress and stability. Kenya was once a major market for slave traders from the Arabic and Middle Eastern countries from the 7th Century into the early and middle 1900's. It was 1963 before Kenya moved from being a British colony to full independence with self-government. Thus, much of the British customs and legal practices remain. To the official English language, the new Republic of Kenya also adopted its native Swahili. The average income in recent years as reported at only $3000 per person. And, of course, the city dwellers are at the high end of the scale with their jungle counterparts often in severe poverty. Kenya is not a land of prosperity

My personal service to the missions team in 2011 was in one-on-one evangelism, speaking the Gospel story and sharing tracts at every opportunity. Of course, other team members ministered with me, moving through the groups that gathered and speaking with individuals. We gave out over 700 tracts and over 100 Bibles in the Swahili language. And with every one, we were able to make personal contact and offer spiritual help.

Much of the work was with existing orphanage and hospital outreaches. The climate and sanitation are such that infections were not just common among the children. Infection seemed to be the norm. Pneumonia among the little ones was rampant. Most days our medical workers saw to the children's health needs as others of us were busy feeding them and teaching them the stories of Jesus.

A defining time for me was a walking ministry though the slum community of Kibera. Within a 10 mile radius, over 700,000 people seek a piece of cardboard or tarp to cover their small square of space. It is basically a garbage dump ... a maze of alleyways, garbage piles and cesspools. We walked daily through the shacks, witnessing house-to-house, talking with those who would hear us. If we had not had a local person from the area who knew the way through the labyrinth, I would probably still be wandering there today.

Our goal is always the ministry of the Gospel but the Bible is clear when it comes to the physical needs of the poor among us.

> "If anyone has material possessions and sees his brother in need but has no pity on him, how can the love of God be in him? Dear children, let us not love with words or tongue but with actions and in truth." (1 John 3:17-18)

We are responsible for 1 John 3:17-18 just as we are responsible for any other part of the Bible.

It was wonderful to distribute over 200 pairs of reading glasses and watch the people smile as they found they could see to read their Bibles again. I just wish I had taken more with me. Always, always, we wish we had more to give.

Kenya has had solid missions work for many years, and the church facilities, hospitals and orphanages show the dedication of local ministers and workers to carry the Gospel. Inside church buildings or standing on open-air platforms, I always had an attentive congregation. The

Kenyan church leaders were doing a good job but were anxious to learn to do it better. We bonded as one family in the Lord, discussing ideas and trying to find new and better ways to do things.

But, this trip to Kenya had special meaning for me. I had prayed for 26 years for an opportunity to minister to the Maasai people. Why I was so concerned to present the Gospel to this particular group, I do not know. But, it never left my heart. The trip to Kenya brought an answer to my prayer. I asked among the church people until I found a guide to a tribal village some six hours out of town. It was a long, dusty trip into the Sahara over a terrible desert road. The Maasai have long been the tribal owners of the large Sahara area in Kenya but now face problems as current governments try to squeeze them out of their land in order to insert large ranches and touristic developments. The nomadic Maasai are gradually losing their hunting lands, a real threat to their historical life style which centers on the hunting of wild game.

I wondered if we would find hostility or objection to our visit because of this situation. We stopped at the entry of the village and awaited the chief and his permission to enter. He greeted us with kindness and offered access to his people and time to speak with them.

Housing was a cluster of crudely constructed huts of mud and stick. Though not aromatic, the roofs of cow dung were very effective against the desert wind and water. Rain is rare in the area, but when it does come, it is a torrential downpour. No windows or light were in the houses, and only one door was allowed. Mosquitos here were numerous and carried disease. Everything was structured to leave as little access as possible for such creatures. Within the dark house was a single room with places for sleeping and one corner dedicated to cooking. In that corner only, a smoke section to the outside was devised. We were treated to a display of tribal dance and drums. The warriors appeared in native apparel and began to dance. They leaped and jumped as we watched in amazement. Obviously leaping high was a great skill. It was a contest to see who could go the highest, who could be the most dramatic.

I was privileged to speak to the entire tribe at the invitation of the chief. In a central place, the people gathered and listened as I spoke. I knew they were a "blood sacrificing" people, incorporating the slaying of animals and the pouring out of blood in their primitive religious worship. As I held up a tract showing Jesus on the cross, I emphasized the blood that flowed freely from His side. In that manner, I gave understanding of salvation to each of them through the blood of Jesus. I finished with the question, "Do you understand what I have told you today?" The response was a clear "yes" and all of the tribe repeated the sinner's prayer with me.

"Why?" I asked the Lord after our return to the city. "Why did it take 26 years for my prayer to be answered?" The response of the Lord was clear in my spirit. They would not have been ready to hear my message before then. I had to await the Lord's place and the Lord's timing. The Lord goes before us. He prepares the way. He gives us a desire for service, but we must trust Him to bring it to pass in due season.

Medical Clinic

> *Much of Rev. Skelton's missions ministry has been in church planting, preaching, teaching leadership skills, and mentoring local workers. But in the midst of these tasks, he has participated in almost 100 medical missions. So, perhaps we need to look at just how a "Medical Mission" works.*

The clinics are under the joint leadership of White Fields Missions, La Ceiba, Honduras, and Omega Medical Missions, Lake City, Florida. The leaders are in charge of selecting and planning for each clinic trip. Most clinics are held in Central American countries, though some extend to the Philippines and Thailand. Let's see how the "normal" clinic runs.

Getting started:
-- Set the dates and countries for clinics.
-- Send out the call to all who would want to participate.
-- Reserve hotels and transportation (buses or vans, arrange drivers).
-- Set the locations of clinics with local church groups.
--Get medicines that can be transported into target area.

Cost of trip:
-- Participants arrange and pay for own airfare.
-- Project fee varies at times but is usually near $775 per person, paid to project leaders upon arrival. These funds

cover housing, transport, some meals, and other project expenses for the week.
-- There are occasions when an offering is taken for a special situation. These offerings are voluntary and private.

Who is coming?
-- "Come ye all." Everyone can find a way to serve so all are welcome.
-- Medical personnel, interpreters, a set-up crew and crowd directors, workers for pharmacy, distribution of eye glasses, and in children's ministry as well as leaders for spiritual clinic are needed.

What kind of people do this?
-- Be "Flexible" and "don't complain" is the motto of the team. There is no time for "drama" on these trips.
-- Enthusiasm and kindness are critical for work made stressful by long hours, dust and dirt, heat, and sometimes a lack of appropriate supplies.
-- Generosity required -- It is a "self-pay" project with participants arranging air fare and paying a sum to cover housing, and other expenses.
-- Ability to change ideas, attitudes, and jobs. It may take a trip or two to find one's "niche". The more familiar one is with the clinic process, the more tasks he or she can do.
-- Age doesn't matter. Accompanied children up to senior citizens all find things they can do.
-- Keep on coming! Most participants find the experience life changing and many return again and again.

Arrival and Clinic prep:
-- Meet all necessary flights and get everyone to hotel with luggage (hopefully).
-- Set up orientation meeting.
-- Arrange currency exchange and payment of project cost.
-- Sleep and be ready for medicine prep on Sunday afternoon. Medicines must be counted, repackaged, and properly labeled. These are then divided into daily allotments and packed into suitcases or boxes for transport.

First day of clinic:
-- Since every day is a different location, every day is a "1st day".
-- Be up, fed and ready to travel by 8 a.m. Help carry out the supplies and load them on top of the vans.
-- Squeeze into a small space between two other people and try to rest for the hour or more trip on country roads. Don't look at the mud slides, or the cliff sides, or the traffic.
-- Wait! Upon arrival, the first ones in are the "set up" people. Every place is different and the clinic stations have to be decided every day. Once those decisions are made, each group sets up the clinic stations as follows:
    A. Registration
    B. Spiritual Clinic
    C. Waiting area for health services
    D. Consultation tables
    E. Pharmacy
    F. Eye Glass Distribution
    G. Children's Ministry

How needs are met:
--Spiritual Needs: Clients receive a brief presentation of the message of salvation plus individual prayer. A Bible or New Testament is also given.
--Health Needs: Clients take their registration paper (one per family) to a medical table where a doctor or nurse (with interpreter if needed) discusses individual needs and problems. Appropriate medications are prescribed. The medical recommendation is sent to the pharmacy to be filled while clients proceed to eye glasses if needed or to wait for medications.
--Pharmacy: Medical orders are filled and placed in separate bags. The "verifying table" reviews the bag to be sure all medications are as ordered. Medicines are then distributed to clients with verbal instructions if needed.

The most common medical needs:
-- Vitamins and parasite medication are given to all appropriate clients
-- Muscle pain, headaches, coughs, nasal congestion are most common
-- Infections receive antibacterial medications with careful instructions. Urinary and pulmonary infections are the most common.
-- Open wounds are encountered and dealt with by qualified personnel.
-- Almost every week of clinic will have one or two clients with serious conditions needing hospitalization or local medical referral. These cases are handled and followed up by local church leadership with guidance from the medical team on hand.

Finishing up for the day:
-- Repack all meds in the pharmacy
-- Return all property borrowed or used during clinic
-- File registration papers and medical orders
-- Load supplies and equipment back on the van or bus
-- Collapse into a seat, grab a cold drink of water, and try to talk about the day
-- Unload all boxes and supplies at the hotel and prepare those needed for next day
-- Attend a general meeting to discuss day and have devotional
-- Out to dinner as you wish and get some sleep because tomorrow is an early start again

Benefits to participants:
-- Knowing you have done service in the Lord's kingdom in caring for those in need
-- Learning about other people and cultures, and how to respond to stress and things that are unexpected.
-- Fun Day: One day of the week is a rest day, usually mid-week. A selection of activities are made available which may include hiking up a volcano, doing a historical tour or just sleeping late and relaxing for the day. And, of course, souvenir shopping is always just around the corner.

The first stop for clients at the clinic is "Spiritual Clinic" with Rev. Skelton. With the help of trained workers and local ministers, he presents the Gospel story and offers prayer opportunity for both salvation and healing. Then comes interviews with medical personnel, eye glass evaluation, and the issuing of medications.

Lines from Louise...
Louise tells that she was in charge of spiritual clinic on the first medical missions trip. Then when Hugh saw what she was doing, he commented, "Hey. I can do that." With her job taken, Louise moved on to interpreting and eventually to managing the eyeglass table. At age 88, Papa Hugh sees more than 400 people in his spiritual clinic each day of the trip while Louise helps them see better.

The Statistics as of 2017:
On average, 350-400 persons are seen per day in each of four clinics per week. Conservative reporting for the past 18 years indicates:

Clinics held:	103
Clients treated	148,000
Salvations reported	25,000
Volunteer workers	2,000+

In addition, hundreds of pairs of eye glasses have been distributed as well as toys and treats for children, and sometimes food or clothing. All of this is done by volunteers who choose to serve.

MEXICO

"No weapon formed against thee shall prosper ..."
(Isaiah 54:17)

South of the border ... down Mexico way! It's familiar territory for Louise, Allen, and myself since we spent 10 years living just across the border in south Texas. It all began with a Sunday School. Louise would pull out her accordion and her flawless Spanish, find a backyard or a patio and start the work.

> *Lines from Louise Skelton ~~*
> *Sunday School provides a perfect tool for involving children in Christian teaching. My first task was always to find a place for teaching. In Mexico, it was the patio of a family interested in church work. Their daughter helped me in the door to door invitation for children to come to Sunday School. I walked through the neighborhood, inviting the children to our meeting. We started with simple songs. My accordion fascinated them. Then we progressed to Bible stories illustrated with flannel board cut outs. I also tried to have a piece of literature for them to take home from each session. It was the first step toward the establishing of a church.*

This was a common process in starting a new mission effort. Louise would start with the children in Sunday School. We would advance to a rented building and Sunday morning services, and then build a church. Though I preached on occasion, my missions philosophy has always been to develop local leadership and ministry. Soon we were having steady

Sunday morning services, added some musicians, and eventually had enough congregation to build a church. Our first church in Reynosa was built with the financial help of a group in McAllen, Texas. The result was a truly fine building that would become our headquarters church in Mexico. Services included Sunday School, Sunday worship, and additional classes for children and young people. A local Mexican pastor took over the leadership and the missons effort in Mexico was well underway.

We began our outreach in the area with one worker, a young Bible School student named Jose Rubio. Jose came straight from Bible School. He had a minimum of training but a bundle of intelligence and dedication. The success of our missions in Mexico owes much to his leadership. Today he is a respected leader in our Texas and Mexican churches.

One of our first ministries in Mexico was in the prisons of Reynosa. As with many countries, the prison system there is not at all on par with the prisons in the United States. Prisoners are not given proper food and clothing but must depend on family gifts for even the basic necessities for survival. Our only worker in that first year or two was Jose. He knew the street life well from experience and preached often in the prison. One day, after he had finished speaking, a prisoner approached him. "It's easy for you to say those things about Jesus because you have a shirt on your back. I don't even own a shirt." Jose left the prison that day without his shirt. He had pulled off his shirt and handed it to the man who had none.

Contacts farther south in Morelia, Mexico, led to several churches in that area, and it eventually became the location of our Bible School as well as a center of strong leadership in the Mexican conference. Those were the days! Days when we could travel easily throughout Mexico, enter with almost no paperwork, and feel relatively safe. From our summer sessions at our Missionary Training Center, we took groups of students and future missionaries into the country to work with churches and to experience true mission work.

That freedom of travel no longer exists. Outside of the touristic Yucatan peninsula, Mexico has become a very dangerous country. Drug lords hold control of most areas, and Morelia has become the "central control" for drug business in the country. The son of one of our pastors was kidnapped by gangsters in Morelia. He was released unharmed after three days. His safe return was certainly due to prayers and the work of the Lord on his behalf. Fortunately, that danger is abating, and our pastor there says he feels safe to walk the streets most evenings now.

It was in Morelia that we established our Bible School which has been a major factor in the growth of the work throughout the country. Young people from all parts of the country come to study and to minister in the area during their stay. They are intelligent, courageous men and women, dedicated to ministry.

Our Bible School Director had a great burden to minister among the large population of Tarascan Indians who populate that area, but such an outreach was difficult. Outsiders were not welcomed by the secluded villagers. In fact, it was dangerous to enter the area. How could the students get access to teach the Gospel? It would take a unique plan, and Jose Rubio came up with an idea truly unique. He knew that the military was accepted everywhere in Mexico. To gain access to the inaccessible villages, he simply formed the students into ministry teams and supplied them with uniforms that resembled the military. It changed everything. Suddenly their visits were acceptable. Their teaching and preaching received considerate attention. Churches began to spring up in several villages that had before been off limits. It was an unusual plan that led to the establishing of a permanent ministry among the Tarascans.

The mission work in Mexico centered in the border town of Reynosa and in Morelia, a good 10 or 11 hour drive (900 miles) into the country. Jose was raised in that area of the country, and we were blessed to join efforts with Rev. Jose Arroyo and his family. He and his brother were not young men but had been in ministry for many years. With the help of the Arroyos, we began a treacherous contact with isolated tribes of Tarascan Indians in lower Mexico. Brother Arroyo went often into the Tarascan areas to preach the Gospel, often having to swim a river to escape harm from those opposing him. But, he was "no quitter". He continued to press into the unknown.

As we gained converts among them, we built churches ... small cement block buildings. On one occasion, we went for service and found some village men had taken picks and shovels and torn the building completely to the ground. No stone was left upon the other. Our response was to simply rebuild the church. A strong Christian congregation now worships there.

Twice, I saw sacks of rocks waiting for me in Tarascan villages. Once, we took a group of North Americans and local Christians to La Luz to dedicate a church. We arrived to see the church surrounded by men with sacks of rocks on their backs. A man with a double-barreled shotgun stood at the front door of the church. Brother Arroyo talked with the men and then to me. "They will not permit the service," he said.

My response was clear, "If we don't dedicate the building, we might as well close the work in this area."

"You don't understand, Brother Hugh. They intend to kill you if you go on with this dedication."

I had no hesitation. "I counted the cost before I first left for the mission field many years ago, Brother Arroyo.

If I have to lay down my life for the Gospel work, I already made that commitment."

Local church leaders had begun to gather with us as we talked. Our North American guests spoke no Spanish and had no idea what was happening. But, they knew it was not good. I realized that the front door of the church was blocked, but no one had gone to the back so I led the group around the building and we entered there. As we entered the building, I asked them to start singing choruses of praise and worship. They continued to pray and to sing as I dedicated the church and delivered my sermon. That day I spoke with as great an anointing of God's Spirit as I have ever experienced.

We left the church in a line formed with one local person, one visitor, one local person, one visitor, etc. Our path led us directly through the group of rock carriers. Our van was parked over on the road, past some corn fields. As we made our way back through the fields, we caught glimpses of men hiding among the corn stalks. They had their bags of rocks. At the van, it was no surprise to find a flat tire. It was just another way to deter us, to frighten us, to make us give up our ministry there. I asked the group to gather in a circle around the van and sing choruses as our friends changed the tire. We left the village with not one rock thrown and not one shot fired.

On another occasion, Brother Arroyo and I went into a village to preach and to stay overnight. In the early morning hours, he awoke and felt in his spirit that we must leave immediately. At 2 a.m., we gathered our things. We heard and saw the stones that were thrown our way, but none hit us. The weapons "formed against us" did not prosper. They did not find their mark.

I was not present when a lady witch doctor was encountered in a Tarascan village. Brother Arroyo approached on a Saturday afternoon with the intention of preaching to the people when he saw her standing in the middle of the community. She was teaching voodoo practices. His first thought was to step forth and challenge the teachings. But, a spirit within directed him to wait. He was not strong enough spiritually to face these forces but was to go home and fast for a week. The next Saturday, he returned to the same scene and stepped into the group to speak the truth of God's Word. As he spoke, the people were moved to repentance and began to pray with him. Even the witch doctor found Christ that day. She was the first of the village to join the church that grew from this meeting, and years later she would become very important to my life. It is always important to wait for God's timing when doing God's work.

I later had a problem not in Mexico but in Columbia, South America, as a fellow minister and I had a stopover on our way to Brazil. I became exceedingly ill and wound up in a hospital late in the night. I was unable to continue our trip. But, there was no medical help for me. Columbian doctors found my heart condition too frightening for them to attempt any medical treatment. I had lived with that heart problem since birth, but any medical person who heard the slushy sound that should have been a firm beat from my chest was startled. They did not want to have any responsibility in case the "gringo" died. I returned to my hotel and continued to Brazil the next day. As our missionary couple there greeted us, the wife said, "You were sick last night, weren't you? The Lord woke me at 3 a.m. to pray for you." Several months later I was visiting with my uncle in Florida, and he asked me to remember a specific date some months past. On that night, the Lord woke me at 3 a.m. to pray for you." It was the date of my hospital visit in Columbia. The story does not end. It was several years later that I was visiting the Tarascan village in Mexico. The former witch doctor become church leader approached me. "Several years ago, were you very sick? The spirit of the Lord woke me in the early morning to pray for you." The Lord is indeed amazing. I was sick and unable to get medical care in a country where we had no church friends. And the Lord woke up three people in three different countries to intercede on my behalf. How can I not put Him above all others and His work above anything I would desire?

Of all the places I visit in Mexico, there is none that attracts me so much as Janitzio. It is an island in Lake Patzcuaro about an hour from Morelia. There the local fishermen gather the small silver white fish popular in the area with picturesque butterfly nets. They are the fishermen seen on the cover of *Vision Caster*, the book about my early missions work. The population of less than 2000 live in homes clinging to the steep hillside beneath a gigantic statue of Mexican hero, Benito Juarez.

Our first visit was nothing more than a tourist visit to a unique area. But, I just don't go anywhere without thoughts of missionary opportunities. Life is not a "challenge". It is an opportunity, and I am always looking for that moment. When I learned there were no Protestant churches on the island and that the local Catholic Church forbade Bibles among the people, I knew this was something I must address. I felt a call within my spirit to bring an open Gospel to these people. We took our boat back to the mainland where I emptied my camera case.

I filled the case with New Testaments and declared that I was ready to make my return. Getting there was easy…but what should I do with the Bibles? I did not want to get people into trouble. Yet, I knew they needed access to the teachings of Jesus. In mid-afternoon, I sat in a restaurant and ordered a coke. As I drank it, the owner struck up a conversation with me, and I asked, "Are you Catholic?" His immediate response was "no". He had worked in the States for several years and had become an evangelical, a member of the Assemblies of God Church. When I told him what I had brought, he asked me to leave the Bibles with him. There were other Protestant Christians on the island that needed them. He would be sure they were distributed properly. Again, the Lord amazed me by preparing the way before me so I might accomplish His work.

In years to come, two young people from the island attended our Bible School in nearby Morelia. When they finished their studies, they returned and opened a church in a building owned by their father. It was allowed because their families were members of the island community. The small camera case of New Testaments matured into an active church in Janitzio.

My more recent visits to Mexico have allowed me to sit back and enjoy watching the work of competent dedicated pastors. To be honest, I am no longer needed to help them run their conferences. I am a privileged guest enjoying dinners and conversations with the sons of the pastors I worked with 50 years ago. Praise and blessings to the fine leadership in Mexico.

My journeys there for the past few decades have been to dedicate churches, to attend conferences, or to be a part of some celebration in the church. The yearly youth conference has brought 1500-2000 young people together from Central America and Texas. A large Ladies Auxiliary works through Central America and often attends our annual U.S. conference in Georgia. They have even begun a publication ... a really nice monthly magazine "Avianza", covering the Spanish-speaking work and articles of interest to them.

Churches that grew from the Mexican churches cover South Texas also. One of our churches in San Juan, Texas, accepted a challenge to build a "sister church" in the Ukraine. A mission church giving to build another mission church in a distant land! The foundation of good works has been taught as clearly as Christian ethics and doctrine.

The glory goes to God. The work was done by men and women whom He anointed for the task. We cannot think of Mexico without pride in our "other son", Jose Rubio and his wife, Mary. They have shown the way and given their entire lives to this work. In Cuba, Jose has been our contact person for many years. He traveled to Havana to meet with our Cuban Superintendent during the years when no American was allowed. For their 50th anniversary, Louise and I sent both Jose and Mary to Havana to celebrate.

From the beginning with Louise's Sunday School, through dangers from rocks and guns, and after thousands of miles of travel, we find a solid, progressive work in Mexico. Today there are over 400 churches in the country that have spread over the border to the establishing of a major conference of Spanish-speaking churches in Texas. Spirit-led action by the people of Mexico has brought a harvest of souls.

NICARAGUA

What was your "God moment" for today?

Jump up and down! Jump up and down! Our medical team had all gathered to the back of our bus and were jumping in the air and landing with as much power as our bodies would give. Well, we were stuck in the mud in the middle of rural Nicaragua, and that was the best we could do. It worked. We did get out of the mud, and we did get back to our hotel. It was a quick shower and early to bed with grateful hearts and tired bodies.

Nicaragua, the largest country of Central America has probably proved to be one of the most unstable. From its Spanish colony status, Nicaragua passed through several unions with other countries, a hot/cold relationship with involvement of United States Marines and a more recent period of dictatorships. Names like the Samozas, the Sandinistas vs. the Contras, Daniel Ortega, and even an American mercenary named William Walker leave most Americans confused about who is in power today or who was the man of the hour yesterday. Today the country is governed under heavy Communist influence.

Yet, the church in Nicaragua is active and growing. The evangelistic fire of our Costa Rican churches spread across the border into Nicaragua some years ago. Within the main city of Managua, churches are numerous, and country towns and villages are dotted with small church buildings and congregations. One of our larger churches in Managua operates an elementary school with over 300 students.

Communist philosophies are usually thought of as contrary to church activity, but the government in Nicaragua has adopted a very lenient stand with religious organizations. The history of change and revolution over several decades has led to a government that must avoid contention with groups as large as the Christian community. The support, or at least the lack of open opposition, is critical to maintaining power for the government. And, the churches pursue the task of winning souls rather than taking control of the government. However, the term "religious freedom" has its limitations. Every evangelistic effort must be approached with caution, and Nicaragua is no exception.

I travel to Nicaragua almost yearly for our church conference. Strict gun laws and rapid punishment of criminals make it one of the safer countries in Central America. No guns are allowed in the major cities. I am amazed at the economic growth over the past few years with an influx of malls and fast food businesses.

Mass crusades are especially effective in Nicaragua. Most recent statistical reports show over a million evangelical believers in over 7000 churches. The church has advanced to the stage that my greatest task at their conferences is just to give advice when asked and to enjoy their fellowship. If believers will step up to share the Gospel on a personal level, the country will see tremendous growth spiritually.

Nicaragua is fairly easy to visit these days, but it has not always been so. In the past, revolution and rebel insurrection have openly intimidated people throughout the countryside. Many a road trip would lead us into dangerous territory with rebel road blocks and soldiers carrying automatic weapons. It took a lot of prayer to even get up nerve to go into the rural areas. On one occasion in Nicaragua, we got a bit too far into the area of conflict. A military group stopped our vehicles and was so concerned about the danger of travel that they asked us to spend the night in their barracks for safety. We certainly did not argue with them but spent the night on military bunks and continued on our way at daylight. Did we enjoy it? No, but we were thankful for the night of safety.

Other ministry trips are to villages some distance outside of Managua. There the "city life" is like another planet. Life in the remote areas is harsh. Most live in thrown together shacks without clean water, medical supplies, and adequate food. The people are always responsive to our ministry, but I am most touched by the children. They are so desperate for attention and for what we have to give them. And, being like all children, they delight in the few toys we might have with us. Thankfully, missionaries and churches working in the local area have begun to be concerned about the situation and are making efforts to bring long lasting relief to the area.

My most recent trip to Nicaragua brought me to the home of an old friend. The former Superintendent of our Costa Rica churches had moved to work with the Nicaraguan church. Having known the couple for over 44 years, I was amazed at their move from city life in Costa Rica to a mountain area of Nicaragua. After a wonderful reunion with them, they took me to the only hotel in town, providing me with the best they could find. However, if the hotel were to be "rated", it would not even make the charts. I asked immediately for extra blankets as I prepared for a very cold night in a sparse room – two single beds – nothing more in the room. I realized that my friends were doing all they could for me. They treated me with the utmost respect. Still, I was not displeased when a Managua minister came to drive me back to the city and better lodging the second night.

It was humbling to see how a couple with years of experience and leadership experience had given up their nice home and life in one of the most prosperous countries of Central America to come to a mountain church of poverty. They had already taken the church, which had dwindled to 5 members, forward to over 35 members in just a few months. They will succeed. Their dedication will bear fruit as the church is nourished by their experienced ministry and love for the people.

On another occasion, we made a trip to Nicaragua with a group of friends who had visited the country before and were involved in medical clinics with local churches ... churches far out of town. I went as the official interpreter. Rain, dirt roads, and stuck vehicles pretty much describe our travel. Far from the big city, we stayed in a "compound" for much of that week, holding daily clinics for the local people. It was not the most comfortable of places, but it was adequate. After completion of the clinics, we returned to the capital city of Managua for a few days where I experienced my "God Moment' of that trip.

I had been rather displeased with myself in that I had failed to contact the Superintendent of our church work in Nicaragua on this trip. I wanted to visit with him and get the latest church news. He was a good friend but somehow I had come without even bringing contact information on how to reach him. This neglect on my part bothered me. But, one day, as I was riding a public bus in Managua, a car pulled up beside us and began blowing the horn furiously. I ignored it until a fellow passenger touched my arm and said, "I think that man is trying to get your attention."

Yes! The car horn was for me. It was the man I had thought I could not find. It was the church Superintendent whose address and phone number I had left at home. Somehow, he had looked up at the bus and recognized me through the window. I immediately asked the bus driver to stop and let me off. I climbed into my friend's car with total joy. He was kind enough to stay and help our group the rest of the week so we could enjoy one another's company. Miracles ... even seeming small ones ... do happen. That night at our regular group session, we were to tell our "God Moment" for that day. There was no doubt as to what mine was. In a city of over a million people, I had found the one person I most needed to see.

NIGERIA

Witches and spiders

Road block again. It must have been the fourth in two hours. Soldiers in camo outfits lazily eased themselves from their vehicle, took up their automatic weapons, and headed our way. Usually it only took a quick look in the open trunk and a glance at our travel documents. But we could see other travelers, mostly locals, pulled to the side of the road for a thorough search and questioning. We were never threatened or treated rudely, but these stops were an annoyance. And, the display of guns was always unsettling.

We were in Nigeria for a city revival campaign in the city of Enugu. Our first stop was Lagos. The metropolitan area Lagos is the largest city on the African continent, and one of the fastest growing cities in the world. It's location as a port city on one of the world's largest deltas makes it a center of trade and commerce for all of Africa. While the largest church in the world is in the lower area of Nigeria, the northern part of the country is a different story. The rivalry of local tribes has plagued the area for years and often takes the form of resistance and persecution of evangelical efforts. Churches have been burned and Christians killed by Muslim opposition to the Gospel. As with most countries, the hard places are the most in need of spiritual awakening.

At least, we didn't have a language problem here. Since the country has over 300 different tribal groups, English has been made the "official language". It is not spoken by all people all of the time, but it is generally understood by all groups. So, the language is the easy part of Nigeria, a country of upheaval and governmental chaos. When I arrived in 2012, they had finally evolved to a relatively democratic government which would pave the way for a successful future.

The flight into Lagos was not particularly bad, but it was long. Nigeria is just a long way from my home in Gainesville, Georgia. We were instantly recognized as foreigners as we came out of the airport and were greeted by a witch hurling curses at us. Though much of Nigeria is very open to Christianity, tribal religions and more primitive activities still make their appearance. Revival among university students has led to great church growth recently, but killings and church burnings by Muslim opposition have taken a toll. The witch's curses were probably more troublesome than the roadblocks to be encountered on the way to Enugu.

The trip to Enugu was a dangerous one. It was here we had to stop so often at the military roadblocks for inspection of our papers and our belongings. In later services, we would find a large guard group, heavily armed and tasked with assuring order among the crowds. This sounds extreme, but Nigerian history is marked by violent government changes. One tribal group would take power and enjoy the money and power of a corrupt government for a few years. Then, another group would rise to power with the same goals of greed and personal enrichment. They were at last establishing a solid government with effort at true democracy. The new government was intent on changing the corruption and financial graft policies of the past. As with all countries in transition, in 2012, Nigeria had not arrived at that goal, but it was on its way.

The campaigns in Enugu followed a similar pattern. It included daily radio shows, daily evangelistic services, and huge evening crusade services. On many occasions, there were over 120,000 in the night services. Who do you think counted them? No one. It was explained to me that mathematically, the officials had determined how many people could stand in what we would call an "acre of land". Then, they just multiplied that number by the amount of land the crowd took up each evening. The intelligence and creative thinking of the people is amazing.

One day in Enugu, I became violently ill with food poisoning. And, it was my day to deliver the sermon at the daily service. I felt too sick to get out of bed. I simply could not get ready to go. But, one among our group would not allow it. He literally forced me to get out of bed and dress for my task. I could barely walk into the church. As I entered, the people immediately recognized that I was not well. Without guidance, they began to gather and pray for me. Instant healing – a miracle! I was supernaturally strengthened to preach that day. After much of a night and day in sickness and almost without strength to walk to the pulpit, I was energized and lifted up into a spiritual realm that allowed me to deliver the Word of God.

The campaign in Enugu lasted three days. We would then return to the States by way of Lagos. On the trip of the witch's curses, we were subjected to a second attack. She knew where we were staying and had placed several brown recluse spiders in various hotel rooms. My hotel partner and I were both bitten by the spiders. I arrived home in intense pain and was in danger of losing the infected foot that had been bitten.

But, how could I stop then? I was due in to leave for the Ukraine to teach in a Bible college in just a few days. As my local doctor listened to my travel plans and looked at my foot, he remarked "I don't recommend you go anywhere. Do you get my drift?" I simply looked at him and smiled. The next weeks saw me constantly elevating that foot … in the Ukraine.

PANAMA

"There are souls to rescue, there are souls to save. Send the light." – Hymn by C. Gabriel

Panama is an exciting country, but it is more than just a canal and a place where Americans used to be. What you find there depends on your purpose for being there. It stands between two continents, between two oceans, between prosperity and poverty. It also stands between lifeless traditional religion and vital Christianity. The canal, built by French and then American engineers with labor from the islands of the Caribbean, makes it a vital link to international trade. "The Ditch" as it is known makes Panama almost an essential stop for business interests worldwide. It is fascinating to see huge ships passing through the narrow waterway. It is challenging to see the spiritual needs of a population of over 4 million.

This "ditch" also makes it a land of diverse nationalities mixed with multiple indigenous tribes. English is common, beaches are full, and the capital city dazzles with the skyscrapers and freeways. But, there are still a rain forest, jungle communities, poverty and educational need. Panama does not always live up to the glamour of its first impression.

Since 1997, there has been a spreading prayer movement in Panama. The diversity of people and rising wealth of the country have led to moral decay of their religious commitments. Some indigenous tribes in the area of the Columbian border have actually run missionaries out of the area with threats of physical harm.

The spread of prayer for and from within Panama is key to spiritual unity among the churches to combat these spirits of adversity.

I have made numerous trips to Panama to teach and train pastors there. But, a large number of my trips have been on medical missions with my son and a team of doctors, nurses and translators. We conduct clinics in rural areas. We are blessed to have an excellent superintendent of the churches there who helps set up all our missions locations and any other ministry appropriate to our group. This makes our trips pleasant, but the effort to bring spiritual truth and deliverance to the people is always a challenge.

I saw the woman who sat on the front bench showing obvious distress on her face. She was a woman suffering inside. No one knew her, but she sat throughout the service, listening to the singing and the preaching with intent interest. As the close of service, she asked to speak a few words, and we gladly allowed it. Her story shocked everyone. Over the past years, she had made several attempts at suicide so her family would not suffer because of her. As she told her story, it was clear that evil spirit had overwhelmed her. She was not just a "confused person", she was totally depressed and without hope. She preferred to die and not live.

As we gathered and began to pray over her, we watched her face change from darkness to clarity and then to peaceful joy. She was delivered. Her testimony was that her inner spirit was revived. But no such testimony was necessary as the heaviness of her life lifted, lifted visibly. It was not the same face we had seen at the beginning of service. The congregation rejoiced to see God's Spirit fill the empty vessel from which Satan had departed.

In Panama, we see large crowds for our medical clinics, and many are blessed through the evaluation of needs and distribution of medicines. But, our greatest goal is the salvation of souls. We desire to see a spiritual life of joy and peace more than we desire physical health for them. A normal clinic week will serve about 2000 people with medication, eye glasses, and even food. But, it is the delight of seeing a soul find new life, find hope, find a new vision in life, that warms our inner spirits and sparks new flames of commitment to missions.

On my 76th birthday, I was in Panama. Our clinic was being held on the front porch of a single mother. There was neither church nor school for our clinic, so she opened her home for us. As I ministered to the people in small groups, over 50 received salvation. The next step was to start a church in the village. Our superintendent began to search for property and a way to fund a building. From the one-day medical clinic, a vibrant church grew. There is nothing "small" in God's eyes. Every effort for Him has potential we never imagined.

I am often asked how much longer I plan to keep making these trips. My response, "I'll go as long as the Lord gives me health and strength, as long as the 'call keeps ringing'."

PERU

"Lean not to thine own understanding"
(Proverbs 3:5)

Packing up from a day of medical clinic, we saw four men came out of the jungle carrying a hammock. In it, a man with a mangled foot tried to appear strong but was almost unconscious after the 30 minute trip to our station. His foot was slashed with a wound several inches long. His machete had missed its mark and swiped across his foot. Fortunately, or by the grace of God, we had a surgeon on our team. It is not usual to have a surgeon, but this time we did ... either "fortunately" or by the grace of God.

The wound had been stuffed with grass to stop the bleeding, and our surgeon set to work. Just cleaning the wound seemed to take forever. However, the grass had stopped the loss of blood. With antiseptic cleansing, some stitches, and a bag of antibiotics, the man was carried back into the jungle toward his home by his four friends. There is no doubt the man would have died had we not been there that day. Lives are important, and it is a great day when the Lord allows us to lengthen a man's days. But, it does not compare to the joy of leading a soul to the Great Physician who heals lives. Healing lives is our focus. Preaching the Gospel of Christ is our mission.

Peru is as varied a country as can be found anywhere. Its official languages are Quechua and Spanish. But, even a few years studying Quechua will not fill your needs in Peru. The jungle areas we visit are populated by small native groups living primitively in stick homes raised high to keep the river floods away. One can encounter several languages in a day's hike through the jungle trails. Fortunately, at least one person in any group will usually **be** able to communicate in Spanish.

But "usually" is not "always". The city of Iquitos is the world's largest city with no road access. It sits in the middle of the Amazon basin surrounded by jungle and s accessible only by plane or boat. It was there that I overheard someone on the street mention the "Yagua tribe". I had never heard of the group, but I immediately knew the Spirit was speaking to my heart, "That tribe is your responsibility." I argued, "I have no knowledge of them, don't know where they are or how to get there." The Spirit said, "That is not what I said. I said that tribe is YOUR responsibility."

I know that when the Spirit speaks to me so clearly that I must respond. The search began with the visiting of all the travel agencies in city. But I found no one who knew anything about the "Yagua". Discouragement had set in by the time I entered the last possible agency on my list. The travel agent there knew nothing either, but I noticed a rather large man sitting in a chair in the waiting area with arms crossed over his chest. When I asked my question, the man rose and came toward me saying, "I know the tribe and where it is located. They are uncivilized." He indicated that an isolated tribe of Yaguas lived about an hour and a half from the city, and he could take me there in his speedboat at a cost of $250. With my well-developed bargaining skills, I commented, "That is a lot of money for a short trip." His response, "It is dangerous. I won't go for any less."

We left the next morning and sped down a tributary of the Orinoco River. After an hour and a half, we stopped and waited for permission from the tribal chief to go farther. My riverboat captain made a high shrill call that echoed through the dense jungle area. We waited until a similar call came back. That was our permission to guide the boat through a mass of underbrush and into a clearing.

A very large bamboo building actually sat like a raft in the river. Standing in the doorway was the chief with a 7 foot blow gun. Again, we had to wait for the chief's approval to go farther. I again asked myself, "What am I doing here? He doesn't speak Spanish and I don't speak his dialect. How will I communicate?" The answer was that I could not communicate verbally with him, but I had brought gifts of machetes and mirrors. The Spirit within me said, "He will understand a smile." So I smiled as I gave him the gifts I had brought. He responded with a nod and we were invited (by hand signs) into the building.

It was roomy inside, a necessity since the chief had four wives in the house…each assigned a corner as her living area. What I did not know at the time was that he had eight other wives living in a village area nearby. The open area had a square of sand in the middle with a fish on a string hanging over it. I assumed it was a cooking area but there was no fire. After 30 or 40 minutes of gestures but no conversation, our boat turned back to Iquitos. I simply could not comprehend why I was called to this place.

A year later, I was in Iquitos again. And, of course, I was determined to see the Yagua group. As the Spirit directed me, I gathered a very nice Spanish Bible and some New Testaments. "Why was I doing this when I knew that no one at the village spoke Spanish?" As the saying goes, "It is not mine to question why." With that attitude, I set out down the river with my boatman from the year before.

This time, the bamboo building had been moved from the water to land. And, as we drew near, I was astonished to see two young men come out of the jungle bush dressed very much as I was. They spoke to me in Spanish. In shock, I asked, "Who are you and what are you doing here?" It seems they were sons of the chief who had sent them into Iquitos to learn Spanish for the tribe. They were home on a visit. Then, I knew why I had brought the fine Spanish Bible and the New Testaments.

We approached the house and saw that the chief still held his 7 foot blowgun, but now I could communicate with him. Upon seeing my books, the young men indicated to me that the Yagua had no concept of writing as such. They had only "carvings" to record or preserve events. So, I asked the sons of the chief to translate for me as I presented my message.

"I am a religious man. Do you worship anything?"

"Yes," responded the chief. "We worship spirits. We worship them because they tell us where to hunt and fish."

I presented my books and told him through his sons, "This is a book of 'carvings'. In this book of 'carvings', you will find the Chief of All Spirits of the entire world. You need to worship this Spirit, and He will guide you.

This book of 'carvings' will tell you how to live again after death in this world."

I left the books and my message to return to Iquitos. Since then, I have not been back to the area, but I now understand that the Spirit led me in a seemingly impossible place to do an impossible task. All I had to do was set aside my ideas and my ways and accept that God would show me His way.

On another trip, our group divided into three teams designated as Crusade, Medical and Building. The days were busy. One group ministered to the sick, the crusade team explained the Gospel to them, and the building team worked to build a church. By the end of the week, the team had completed a church and had dug a new well to supply clean water to a village. I must admit I had been a bit shocked when we arrived and saw the people washing clothes and even bathing naked in the river. Now, at least, they would have a cleaner environment and a healthier life.

In medical clinic, the most memorable case was a boy of about twelve. His foot and leg looked rotten from infection. Over five months before, he had been bitten by a poisonous snake. But there was no "local clinic" to go to, no hospital down the road. His suffering from pain was etched on his face. After care from the doctor and medications, he was told to rest the leg. The next day, he came again to the clinic to show us how much better his leg was. Healing was working in his body. Today, I like to think that boy went on to run and play with his friends as normal boys do. I praise the Lord to be a part of a ministry so wonderful!

Even as I walk the streets of my hometown in the United States, I often remember the despair and desperation of people such as the indigenous Peruvians who cannot hope to change their situation on their own. They simply do not have the resources or education. Their lives are difficult past our comprehension. We have the great challenge to open a "great and effectual" door to a better future through Christ Jesus. I am saddened to think of the difficulties they face daily, but I am also filled with inner gladness that the Lord allows me to be a part in reaching out to them.

Peru is a country of wealth in resources, but it is also held captive to dense jungle in the north and east and the soaring Andes Mountains along its west coast. The rapidly growing economy promises a more prosperous future. But spreading that prosperity to the isolated tribes throughout the country will not come easily. The church work there is based in meeting the physical needs of the people as well as their spiritual needs. I carry them in my memory. Maybe one day I will again take a boat down a river to find my Yagua friends.

ROMANIA

"Just around the corner"

Looking for Dracula! Well, not really looking for him since Dracula is a character of fiction, but I did spend some time in Transylvania. And, it was cold! Ask me about Romania and I will answer "It was cold." The area we visited seldom gets above freezing on a winter day. And, the people lack many necessities of life, including heated homes. I have never been so cold, never been more touched by the needs of the people, and never more pleased with the opportunity to minister than I was when among the Romanians.

The country has a modern history of tyranny beginning with its invasion by Germany in World War II, followed by a Communist leadership under the influence of Russia. It has slowly begun a transition into democracy and capitalism. But development is slow. And, in some areas of the population, little progress has been made

It was near Christmas when we settled in Cluj to begin our team ministry, mostly to the Roma people of the area. The Roma are often known as "travelers" or "gypsies". (The work "Roma" refers to a specific minority, not the general population of Romania.) Although they are scattered all over the world, more Roma live in Romania than any other country. Poverty and discrimination are their companions. We settled into a Bed & Breakfast in the city. Our supplies were stored in one room which we spent hours in each night, sorting and packing for the next day.

A van transported us to Roma villages outside of town. Their housing was little more than mud and sticks with a few pieces of scrap tin serving as a roof. A family of 5 or more per room was the norm. They had no insulation against the cold, no central heat, no pantry of food. In the city, there were Roma people who had succeeded in life, but most in the country side lacked education and employment. In the rural areas, they survived with little food and a minimum of warm clothing. We arrived with necessities such as sugar, flour, cooking oil, some fruits, and even matches. We also carried a Gospel message because what the Roma people need mostly is hope.

During the week of ministry, 130 families were given clothes, 40 lbs. of food, 30 lbs. of hygiene supplies, as well as toys and candy for the children. An apple, an orange, or a banana for each person – remarkable the joy of a fresh fruit to people who normally never have such things.

Thirty people from those families accepted Christ. The goal of the trip is to share the Gospel with people. However, we believe that all persons deserve the food and medical assistance we carry with us. The love of the Christian is to all persons of all races, of all nationalities, of all faiths. We draw no lines. We exclude no one.

Each day it seemed to be colder, though I'm sure it was not. We trudged through ice and snow to set up delivery stations. Some greeted us heartily while others stood back and were unsure. One lady came to us to tell us of a family "just around the corner" that was unable to get out and come for the food and supplies. Of course, we gathered the bulky 70+ pounds of food and medicines and divided it into several bundles. Two ladies and I set out for delivery "just around the corner."

We turned that corner and saw nothing ... a field of more ice, more snow. No buildings were in sight. Still, we knew our directions and began walking. After about a half mile of trudging, we spotted the small shack. The people inside were indeed not able to walk through the ice and snow. We distributed our gifts and even sang a chorus for them. Of course, we sang in English which they did not understand. Still, we received handshakes, smiles and words that I'm sure meant "Thank you." It reminded me that it is not always the words we say but the things we do that impress people.

Now, all we had to do was get back to the main camp. And, that was "just around the corner", about a half mile or so. As we struggled along, we began to laugh at ourselves and about the hut being "just around the corner". It became the phrase of the trip. In the van, at dinner, or even on the plane home, someone was always commenting that our goal was "just around the corner".

Eventually a church was built in that area with regular church services. I preached there when it was only a partial structure. The two-story building has since been completed, providing an auditorium for services and large group gatherings, as well as classrooms for smaller community needs.

Back in the city of Cluj, we visited government run orphanages as well as homes for special needs children. At each visit, we were greeted by smiles and special programs. At one facility, they had even learned a song in English for us. The special needs children demonstrated their accomplishments and presented a musical program. Then, we played games with them. Soccer balls rolled about on the floor as a little table tennis and other indoor games gave us a chance to interact with them on a personal level.

Romania is not an easy place for missionary work. It is cold. The people are poor. Discrimination against certain ethnic groups abounds. And, the government assistance programs for the large population of displaced children have barely made a dent in the problem. Romania has great need of evangelism and a spiritual revival. I pray such a move of God for these people is truly "just around the corner".

RUSSIA and the UKRAINE

"Big brother is watching."

Most of my trips to Russia were actually trips "through" Russia on my way to the Ukraine. However, in the early 2000's, our group stopped in Moscow for a service and to produce some video on our ministry there. These were not days of open support for religious activity. Our scheduled meeting hall seated 2,000. With strong local opposition, our congregation numbered only a little over 200. Still, the message is the same whether the congregation be large or small. "Jesus loves you. He loves all people the same. You can have new life in Him."

While in Moscow, we were under constant surveillance by government agents. I know it sounds like a bad movie from the 80's, but they were near us when we went to eat or went shopping. They even stayed at our hotel. It was not a time of trust for tourists. Every district in the city had its own "check point". We had to show our official travel papers, answer questions as to where we were going, our reasons for going, and how long we would be there.

Our effort to film a documentary of our trip was shut down. There would be no video in Red Square. Uniformed police left no doubt that our cameras were not welcome. Our only choice was to set up on the roof of our hotel to complete the film. It was about the only place that no one seemed to be watching us.

But the five trips of ministry to the Ukraine were less stressful. Our host minister had been raised in England but felt directed to move to Kiev to begin missionary work. In his early years there, he suffered frequent persecution and even imprisonment for his religious activity, but those times were passing, and the capital city was now open to a religious campaign in the local soccer stadium. The three nights of service drew masses of people and were very successful.

In the daytime, we visited orphanages for the many street children of Kiev. These were government orphanages and were only a little better than street living. There was little running water in the buildings and extreme conditions of cold. But they did meet a need to get as many of the children off the street as possible. Those left on the street often pulled up manhole covers in the street and climbed into the underground tunnels to huddle near the relative warmth of sewer pipes.

One day, we saw a group of children living under a building. Our efforts to get them to come out and receive our gifts of clothing and food were useless. They lived in fear and had no place for strangers in their lives. Finally a few came, but I will never forget a small girl of seven or eight years who would not come. She huddled beneath the building and cried. Her fear of us was greater than any desire to have our food or gifts. The children were not afraid because we were from another country. They lived in fear of anyone who might abuse them or drive them from what little they had.

On a later trip, I was able to visit an orphanage run by a local church where children were well cared for. It was a well-built structure with proper facilities for the children. James 1:27 of the Bible clearly states that we have a responsibility for the care of "orphans and widows". Though our evangelistic message is far beyond a social doctrine, Christianity also carries a responsibility to help those in need. The love of Christ includes compassion for all people and for all suffering. Our call is not just to the masses in a stadium but also to the individual separated from society by poverty and fear.

- Louise helps with glasses
- Happy on the road
- Orphanage lunch
- Nigerian tribesman

- Travel trials
- Father/Son team
- Aruba by the sea
- Tuk Tuk ride

- Feeding in the cold
  (Romania)
- Teaching refugees
- A friend at the Kremlin

- C.H. Church headquarters, India
- Children at India orphanage
- India celebration

SOUTH AFRICA

"Land in Transition"

I didn't know what to expect of South Africa. It has gone from a nation of strict racial division (apartheid) to a land seeking equality for all its people. The decades of separation into groups defined by color or ethnic history was being set aside. No longer are men and women to be labeled as white, black, coloured or Indian/Asian. All people can walk on any street in town. And though living in culturally similar area still exists, it is not required. The days when a population of less than 10% rules all others have past. Apartheid ended only a few decades ago. I was unsure of how we would be received, and how much animosity from past injustices might still separate the people.

I had been invited to teach in Cape Town at a major leadership conference. Our goal was to prepare local leaders and workers to be more effective in preaching and developing strong evangelistic churches. I was assigned specific topics and was required to submit all teaching materials for approval before I left home. Getting approval was not a problem. We were clearly in South Africa to share the Gospel and to teach church leadership, not to examine political programs.

Our leadership conference was very much in line with the goals of the country. We were proud to be one of the first major church gatherings that included all races as one group. The participants of the conference had committed themselves to embracing the change in their society, to the forging of a new South Africa. Discussion groups fascinated me as past racial conflict became an open topic. It was the "small things" that had created strife. They had lived in jealousy. "That man was wearing a baseball cap, but because of my ethnicity, I had no job to afford such a thing." "I had to walk on my streets and could not go to see the houses in other ethnic areas." It was not the requirement to carry "proper papers" at all times, or even the frequent questioning by police as to one's destination or purpose. It was the everyday small actions of discrimination that wore on the people. I wondered how often we as Christians miss the "small things". Do I see the individuals in my ministry or just the crowds? Do I see the pain carried in the hearts of people or just their outward afflictions?

Groups who had lived in the same cities but had been separated by walls of racism stood as one group in our meetings, sharing ideas and worshipping together. The participants were keen to understand their role in church growth and were not shy about questioning areas where they were uncertain. Ethnic division no longer squelched open debate and cooperative planning. I was impressed not only by the wonder of God's drawing these people together, but also by the people's willingness to leave the hardships of the past to push forward for a better life. South Africans are establishing a new path for their country, a path of brotherhood and cooperation.

The natural beauty of South Africa matches the beauty of is people. Cape Town is the business center of the country with its iconic Table Mountain overlooking the city. The views from atop the mountain are indescribable.

Roads from Cape Town lead around the Cape of Good Hope and along sea coasts, into the interior through the kingdom of Swaziland and on to Johannesburg. Take your choice among the winelands, the archeological sites, the cultural centers, the diamond mines, or the remarkable game preserves. It is a country of wealth and opportunity, ready to take its place in the world as an economic leader.

Nelson Mandela is revered as the first president under the new system of equality, South Africa's first black president rose from 27 years of imprisonment. He has led by example and by Christian values. My great disappointment the trip was not meeting Mr. Mandela. He had planned to visit our conference to receive a specially bound Bible as a gift and speak to our conference. A threat to his life the day before the presentation made his coming impossible. He sent a special aide to receive the gift and speak for him. I missed seeing the man but not the people he led.

The commitment of the church in South Africa must become more than a commitment to church services and sermons. Strong leadership at every level will be required. Harmony between missionaries and church staff is critical. The missionary of South Africa must become more African and less western. Education of church leaders is vital, and attention to the social change cannot be ignored.

I went to South Africa not knowing what to expect. I left expecting great things from an incredible group of young people and church leaders. They face the dangers of modern society which values economic success and material possessions over personal morality and Christian ethics. But, they also have a tremendous opportunity and a strong energy for spiritual revival. The people of South Africa face a unique opportunity to "start over again." It is time to take a fresh look at what has been done in the past and what needs to be done in the future. This means a call to the church to fasting and prayer. I pray for God to raise up powerful Christian leaders to meet the challenge. The church must produce "heroes of faith" for the 21st century challenge in South Africa.

ST. VINCENT – The Caribbean

"Be instant in season, out of season" (2Tim 4:3)

St. Vincent and the Grenadines ... I didn't even know they existed, much less where they were. It was at the Conference of the African Pastors' Network in Atlanta that I first met the main pastor and superintendent of the St. Vincent area. He invited me down to teach leadership and preach in the area churches so Louise and I packed our bags and made plane reservations. The island of St. Vincent itself is one of the smallest of a chain of islands just off the northeast of South America. Our trip to Aruba taught us that all Caribbean islands are not like our beloved Cuba. While Aruba is relatively dry and flat, St. Vincent proved to be a tropical paradise. The hills and mountains gave little room to the flat lands near beautiful beaches. Palm trees and vegetation flourished. It was small and relatively poor, lacking in industry and a large tourist trade. Yet, the people we met were a contented, kind people. It was a place one could stay forever.

Going to a Caribbean island sounded good, especially in February, but getting there and back was the challenge. A flight to Miami is fairly normal, a smaller plane took us to Barbados where we spent several hours with a local pastor and left with an invitation to return for ministry. The plane to St. Vincent was even smaller, and by that time, we were tired of airplanes. Of course, that was not the end of the travel. The churches were scattered throughout the mountains, requiring long slow drives on perilous roads. I still cringe a bit when I think of one long drive through the night, rushing ever upward on a single lane road that clung to the side of a mountain and dropped away totally on the other side. Meeting another vehicle on the road meant someone had to back up and find a passing spot. Fortunately, it was done with good spirit.

We were met at the airport by the local pastor and superintendent of numerous churches on St. Vincent and the nearby island of Bequia. My teaching ministry began quickly, but the next morning meant getting up at 5:15 am to do radio work. The pastor who hosted us owned both the radio and the television station for the island and other islands of the Grenadine chain so there was plenty of "media time." For two hours, I spoke and answered call-in questions. "Be instant in season, out of season", admonished the Apostle Paul (2 Tim 4:2). I've prepared and delivered sermons for 68 years, but these random questions kept me on my toes. At least my years of experience are advantageous in that there are few things someone hasn't asked me about before.

Our main focus for the visit was training in leadership for the local pastors with evening evangelistic services. Each day, we traveled to a different local church on the island. Churches appeared on mountainous roads where we could barely find space to park our vehicle. But the church buildings were neat and beautiful inside, filled with kind, gentle people. A congregation of 200 was not unusual. The travel was difficult, but I felt like I was riding in royal style by the time I met the people at our destinations. St. Vincent culture is vibrant and joyful. The population is almost entirely black, given to generosity and kindness, very spiritual minded, and hard working. Their greatest economic problem is lack of work on the island. Since it does not get a lot of tourist trade, the people are confined to local agriculture and business jobs. The wooden buildings are well kept by a people who struggle financially but take pride in what they do and what they have. We were provided with a delightful bayside house with a wonderful porch to relax between services. Having no large restaurant area (only one McDonalds on the island), we thought Louise would have to cook but a constant stream of church members kept us "overfed" with their daily gifts of food and treats.

For Sunday service, I became a TV star! Luckily, I didn't know we were being televised throughout the island until after it was over. Not knowing kept me from being overcome by nervousness. It was a great service that had plenty of re-runs so I guess I got my preaching done for a week. Louise taught a seminar for a large group of the ladies of the church, but she didn't get to be on TV. On Monday, we took the ferry boat to the island of Bequia to spend a day among the people there and enjoy a wonderful service reporting both salvation and healings.

Services were attended by 150-200 people. Music was fantastic ... guitars too many to count ... special services with emphasis on young people and always the support of the older. The response to the Gospel is what makes all missions work worthwhile. So, it was on St. Vincent. We rejoiced to see an elderly woman make peace with God. In another service, 53 people came forward to pray the sinner's prayer and receive the Lord. It is always an amazing thing to see how people of all cultures, races, and geographic locations can focus and relate to one another in worship of the same God.

So, our return to the U. S. was with tired bodies but uplifted hearts. Well, the heart rate did go up and the delight went down a little when our plane began to fill with smoke somewhere between Barbados and Miami. The passengers were in a state of near panic, and Louise was praying. I was concerned but prayed my usual prayer of "Lord let me live until You are finished with my ministry whether it is in the air or on sea or on land." It is the prayer I pray on every trip and that commitment to the Lord's plans for me gives me comfort and peace in situations that bring fear to others. Our pilot came on the speaker and indicated we were having a problem but "don't worry. I can land on any of these islands if necessary." Well, that was encouraging but not exactly what we wanted to hear. It was soon discovered that the air conditioning system had burned up for some unknown reason. The system was shut down and after 45 minutes of smoke filled cabin, things began to clear. We made a detour landing for a safety check but all was fine mechanically. All of this extended our flight and increased our tiredness, but we arrived home late but safe. There is nothing to compare to flight stress and late nights in airports with limited food options. I hope to return to St. Vincent in coming years … but I don't want to experience that return plane ride again. It was good to go and good to get home!

THAILAND/MYANMAR

"Refugee camps and a Mercedes"

Atlanta to Chiang Mai, Thailand, is a 35 hour trip by air. A stop in Seoul, Korea, gave us a chance to stretch our legs and see a few sights, but it did not make the trip at all easy. The toll on our physical bodies as well as our mental energy did not let up. Upon arrival in Chiang Mai, I headed for bed for sleep and relief from "jet lag". But the next morning, we were up early for a long 6 ½ hour drive to the border of Burma, now known as Myanmar. We would be in the city of Mae Sot, Thailand, ministering to refugees for the next three days.

Myanmar is in the midst of change. A more democratic government had been formed in the past few years, but the suffering of 49 years of harsh military rule had taken its toll on the people. And, though the government is more democratic, it is not necessarily less harsh. Hunger, violence, and a world-known sex trade give people reason to escape the country any way possible. These were the people we came to help.

Never had I seen worse conditions for people to live in than the refugee camps of Thailand/Myanmar. In one area, where the city trash was dumped, we had no building but had to use the hood of our truck as a place to sit patients for physical exams. The poverty is not describable. People live with minimum clothing that they have found among the trash. Children were everywhere, but never without an adult watching over them. An unattended child was a child in danger.

Chiang Mai, a larger city located more to the interior of Thailand, is much more developed commercially and educationally. It is an entry and exit point for international travel to the area of Myanmar refugee camps. I was surprised to find that over 250 missionaries live in the city area where we held a service. It seemed odd that so many missionaries would reside in this "out of the way" city? It was, of course, because the city has acceptable housing and resources for families. It is the primary residence for many who minister in nearby countries which are not welcoming to Christian ministry. These missionaries spend their week in underground churches and return to Thailand each weekend to prepare for the next trip. The Chiang Mai area provides a large western community with schools for their children and fellowship with other missionaries. The weekly trips provide spiritual battle fields for their ministries. The weekends provide safety, rest, and spiritual restoration.

We were blessed to have two established missionaries in Thailand to advise us and direct our efforts. There were camp areas, schools, and several refugee agencies trying to help thousands of displaced people. Our six medical clinics provided basic health diagnosis and medications for men, women, and many many children. We visited five schools, two of which were especially for victims of the sex trade. The director of the school was a young woman, age 24. She was giving her life to help these young people. Whenever I think of Thailand and Myanmar, I think to pray for her and the work she is doing.

Most people of Myanmar are Buddhist. Fewer than 2% are Christians, and the move from an antiquated closed culture into the 21st Century seems to be by-passing the religious route. Increased wealth is leading to complacency and materialism with no passion for God or concern for evangelism. However, we found great spiritual concern for the healing of the spirits of the refugees. One of the schools was directed by a Buddhist, but he invited me to pray with him. This was unusual as the countries of Southeast Asia all rank rather low on the international scale for religious tolerance. He invited me to speak to each of his ten classrooms. It was challenging to find an effective way to present the Gospel. I cannot support Buddhism as a religious belief, but neither can I be insulting to those who follow that system. Presenting Christ is a positive action, a gift. I am called not to tear down but to build up. The students responded eagerly. Over a hundred indicated they desired to accept the plan of salvation for their lives.

While speaking at an orphanage in the area, I noticed a very young girl in one of the group sessions. She listened to me intently. I spoke with care and in simple terms as my interpreter was a Buddhist who was somewhat wary of my message. "Jesus, Son of the living God, loves you." It was a clear and personal message that the young girl took to her heart. Her face was transformed into a smile and a look of peaceful joy. It was my feeling that no one had ever told that child that she was loved. I shall never think of my trip to Southeast Asia without remembering her face.

Another privilege of this trip was to talk with and minister to the missionaries who worked daily in the camps. We often forget that the "minister needs ministry".

Working in such impoverished conditions and giving so much of one's self drains the spirit. I especially enjoy the time to listen, to advise, to pray for and to encourage those fighting in the trenches of spiritual warfare.

We did spend a day or so back in Chiang Mai to recover and prepare for the trip home and managed to get in a few local sights. But, the trip back home was surprisingly just as long and difficult as the travel to Thailand. However at the end of the return trip was a good house, good food, and a good wife.

UGANDA

"My grace is sufficient for thee..."
(II Cor. 12:9)

We drove through the gates to our hotel in Kampala. Surrounded on all four sides by high cement walls, we felt quite safe. Little did I realize that I would travel no farther into the city. There would be no trips downtown, no sightseeing, no souvenir shopping. Kampala was a dangerous place for foreigners. The reign of the tyrant Idi Amin ended years ago, but the pseudo-democracy that now ruled still dealt in mass corruption, torture of prisoners, and child labor. To the North, tribes were at war, with constant border conflicts with neighboring countries.

Our invitation to Uganda had come from a pastor from Kampala during his visit to the states. His home church in Uganda seated 12,000. The mega-church served a congregation of believers fully committed to the Gospel and its teachings. I often travel to the countryside and minister in small villages, but the 5,000 delegates awaiting us at the Miracle Center Cathedral was no "small village group".

We started our Uganda adventure, not with a sermon, but with a press conference. Fifteen major leaders from radio stations, TV stations, newspapers, and city government were present. After announcing details of the meetings to come, we discussed our purpose which was to transform the church from an "issue driven" ministry to a "principle driven" ministry. Our focus was to prepare the church to act on spiritual and Christian principles for everyday life and for handling problems. Each team member was introduced to the media and allowed to express his expectations for the coming services.

I enjoy the personal ministry, but I also enjoy the excitement and pleasure of preaching to the thousands. I led a team of five seasoned ministers in teaching and preaching God's word. The unity of our sermons and classes was amazing. With thousands in the daily teaching sessions and twice that many in the evening services, we experienced a remarkable flow of the Spirit and a divine blend of the presentations by different ministers.

The Uganda experience stands out in my mind for the dedication of the people. Each night, a different person in our ministerial group spoke. On Sunday, seven consecutive services were held. I preached the last one of the evening to a congregation of over 7,000.

The services were a wellspring of worship and praise. Constant prayer prevailed before, during, and after each meeting. The Kampala leader managed the large crowds seemingly without effort. A huge congregation of individuals came together with a common goal...to worship and to learn.

The uplifting experience of worship with the Ugandans was only slightly marred by the presence of guards during all services. But, they were a part of the scenery for every service.

Our daily trip to church always included an armed escort and a different route for every trip. If we took a certain route to the church, we had to drive a different route back to our hotel. And the next day, the routes would again be different. Every day brought new security officers and a new route. I felt no discomfort or fear while with the local ministers or local church people. But outside the church walls, I wondered as to what dangers were just beyond our protective maneuvers.

Uganda is rated, on an international scale, as one of the most corrupt nations in the world. The result is that it is also one of the poorest countries in the world. Local officials post security warnings, advising foreigners of the abundant amount of personal crime and theft, and the dangers of frequent political violence.

Among the common population, Christianity is the largest religious group. Church growth is explosive as the people seek peace and spiritual unity. Still their daily lives are constantly threatened by danger and political upheaval. Uganda is a country in need of deliverance.

Zambia

"For my thoughts are not your thoughts, neither are your ways my ways." (Is. 55:8)

In Zambia, I refused the grub worms and left in a Mercedes. It was not an ordinary trip.

Though Christianity is the major religion of Zambia and the official language is English, it is not an easy country to navigate. English is "official" for legal and business usage. However, it depends on which of the 73 tribal language areas you are in at the moment as to what the people are speaking.

A friend in Wales had invited me to visit with missionaries who had an orphanage in a rather dangerous area of the country near the border with the Republic of the Congo. We landed in Lusaka and rented a van for the six hour trip through country of considerable danger. The only roads were dirt tracks of ruts, and we were stopped frequently for that wonderful check of our "official travel documents" that we have presented in so many places in a multitude of countries. The purpose of the stop was not to check our travel papers. It was an effort to collect tips … a little money to grease the wheel of bureaucracy.

Something that amazed me in our travel was the mass of termite mounds. I had seen the large towers of baked soil in other countries but none like those in Zambia. Standing many times the height of an average man and larger at the base than some houses, the plateau area is a forest of termite mounds.

The orphanage was located in the small village of Mufulira with few stores and scattered houses. Copper mining had been the major industry of Zambia for many years and the collapse of that market left wide-spread poverty. The mines had closed, there was no work, and children were without care.

I spent 10 days in the area training and teaching with pastors in the area and working with the children in the orphanage. I shared leadership methods as well as encouragement with the leaders. With the children, I felt inspired with the idea of a garden, so I taught of a spiritual garden, a place where "good seed" planted would grow good things. To make it realistic to them, I helped the children plant a vegetable garden. We planted seed and talked of the expected results if we tended it well and did not neglect it. Our spiritual garden required the same care and effort. It had to be given regular attention. Their vegetable gardens became like a contest to see who could plant and grow the best one. We also bought some pigs and chickens for them to raise. The activity of the garden and the animals not only supplied their physical needs, but also gave them a clear picture of how their spiritual lives needed constant attention. Before leaving the area, we were able to add a playground area for them.

Zambia has one of the largest orphan populations per capita of any country in the world. The average death rate in the country has climbed from the age of 40 into the late 50's in recent years due to better control of tuberculosis, malaria, and HIV viruses. But it is still an unhealthy country with many unsafe areas. The challenge of the orphanage was the constant a constant lack of funds and the number of orphans in need. We have been able to enroll sponsors for at least 30 or 40 of those orphans.

There are never enough of the basic necessities with food being a dire essential. I lived on bananas, eggs and whatever fruit was available in the market. It was a "cook your own meals" affair. As Louise will tell anyone, I am not famous for my cooking ability so no one was asking me to cook for them. Of course, I was able to manage better than the street food. The grub worms did not appeal to me as they did to Zambian customers.

Our return home by way of Lusaka turned out to be rather "unusual". We rented a van and driver to get us back to the city. On the way, we were stopped by a local policeman. The van driver and policeman recognized each other, and our driver "floored it". The policeman was yelling "stop" and managed to jump into the passenger side of the van, screaming at our driver. It seems the two men had experienced conflict before, and they were not fond of one another. After a hectic mile of wild riding with the driver paying no attention to the policeman, the officer was able to reach and turn off the motor of the van, allowing the vehicle to roll slowly to a stop. My minister friend and I sat in the back seat, frozen in place and unsure of what would come next.

The policeman made a radio call to nearby soldiers who promptly pulled our driver from the van and began beating him. We sat in shock and silence. Eventually, a soldier climbed into the van and drove all of us to the local police station. The beaten driver was taken inside as we sat … and sat … and sat. It was clear that we had to take steps of our own if we were to get to Lusaka and meet our flight schedule. The local minister with us decided we should walk a short distance to the office of the major whom he knew personally. After hearing our story, the major immediately said, "Do not worry. I will get you to Lusaka." Within five minutes, a large black Mercedes complete with driver and air conditioning appeared Instead of the back seat of a well-worn van, we rode in an air conditioned, chauffeured, Mercedes to the airport and were stopped by no one for inspection. It seems that God sometimes has an unplanned way to get us to our destination.

EPILOGUE

The 30 countries featured in this book are by no means the full story. The Rev. Skelton has actually traveled in 85 countries on 5 continents. In Columbia, South America, Hugh and fellow ministers traveled by non-motorized river raft with construction supplies to build a church in the jungle where there were no roads. He found his way to Jamaica from a charity golf tournament in Atlanta. (His golf partner turned out to be a missionary from Jamaica that he had never met before. She invited him to come and minister with her group on the island.) There is no finish to the stories nor to Rev. Skelton's travels. Probably the most difficult part of this book was finding him home enough to give the needed interviews.

Rev. Skelton has always worked through the church organization of his youth. The Congregational Holiness Church had known missionary efforts but no churches were established in the name of Congregational Holiness Churches Foreign Missions until Hugh and Louise opened the work in Cuba. Today the church has churches from 33 countries in its fellowship. Rev. Skelton has been a major factor in the evangelism effort in the vast majority of those countries. The Foreign Mission department of the C. H. Church now considers its churches in other countries to be a total or more than 10,000. Every Sunday more than a million people attend those churches for worship. As the "Founding Father of World Missions", the Rev. Skelton is both amazed and humbled by the work God has wrought.

An unusual aspect of this vast international ministry is the fact that it has been accomplished largely without media such as TV programs or radio broadcasts. Mass meetings have been relatively few. The Gospel has been spread through personal contact and ministry. Almost every national leader with whom he works calls Rev. Skelton "friend". They dine with him, welcome him into their homes, and share their pulpits with him. What does this mean? It means that every individual has potential to change the world just through daily ministry and obedience to God's guidance. It means that you, too, can walk "On the Edge of a Miracle."

Appendix

Significant Events

1949	Graduated: Emmanuel College
1951	1st Mission Trip to Cuba
1952	Marriage: Louise Skelton
1954	Birth of son: Allen Skelton
1954	B. A. Degree: Mercer University
1960	Return to U.S. from Cuba
1963	Move to McAllen, Texas (Missionary Training Center)
1963-91	World Missions Director (Congregational Holiness Church)
1982-87	Director, Center for International Ministries- London
1994-05	Missions Pastor (Free Chapel Worship Center)
1997	50th year of ministry
1997	Award: 50 Years of Service (C. H. Church)
1997	Honorary Doctor of Divinity (Word Vision Bible College)
2004	50th Wedding Anniversary
2004	Walter L. Moon Humanitarian Award (Mercer University)
2003-04	Honorary Degrees: (Covenant Life Seminary) Masters & Doctor of Ministry, Doctor of Divinity
2005	Award: "Founding Father of World Missions" (Congregational Holiness Church)
2011	Open Heart Surgery
2013	Africa Love Award (African Pastors Network)
2016	Life Achievement Award (Pentecostal Holiness Church, Hyderabad, India

The Skelton Family

Starla, Allen, Hugh, Louise, Ryan, Kate, Vicky, Bethany, Koral

Rev. Hugh Skelton can be contacted through:

Missions Support Services
P. O. Box 7021
Chestnut Mountain, Georgia, 30502
MSS.Skelton@yahoo.com

On the Edge of a Miracle can be ordered from the above address as can the first of the Rev. Skelton's books, ***Vision Caster***.